T0266513

Queer Heroes of Myth and Legend

Queer Heroes of Myth and Legend

A celebration of gay gods, sapphic saints and queerness through the ages

Dan Jones

First published in Great Britain in 2023 by Radar,
an imprint of Octopus Publishing Group Ltd, Carmelite House,
50 Victoria Embankment, London EC4Y 0DZ
www.octopusbooks.co.uk

An Hachette UK Company
www.hachette.co.uk

Text copyright © Dan Jones 2023
Design & layout copyright © Octopus Publishing Group Ltd 2023

Distributed in the US by Hachette Book Group,
1290 Avenue of the Americas, 4th and 5th Floors, New York, NY 10104

Distributed in Canada by Canadian Manda Group,
664 Annette St, Toronto, Ontario, Canada M6S 2C8

All rights reserved. No part of this work may be reproduced or utilized
in any form or by any means, electronic or mechanical, including photocopying,
recording or by any information storage and retrieval system, without
the prior written permission of the publisher.

Dan Jones asserts the moral right to be identified as the author of this work.

ISBN 978-1-80419-046-3

A CIP catalogue record for this book is available from the British Library.

Printed and bound in the UK.

3 5 7 9 10 8 6 4 2

Publisher: Briony Gowlett
Senior Editor: Leanne Bryan
Design Director: Mel Four
Illustrator: Jade Moore
Production Manager: Caroline Alberti

Typeset in 11/17pt Heldane Text by Jouve (UK), Milton Keynes

This FSC® label means that materials used for
the product have been responsibly sourced.

For all my heroes (you know who you are)

CONTENTS

INTRODUCTION
We can (all) be heroes

My love of myths and legends springs from one fantastical source: the 1981 epic movie *Clash of the Titans*. At the time of its release, *Clash* stunned reviewers with its Hollywood handling of myth and magic. Roger Ebert reviewed it in the summer of that year, calling it 'a grand and glorious romantic adventure, filled with grave heroes, beautiful heroines, fearsome monsters, and awe-inspiring duels to the death'. But I knew nothing of this when, as a small child, I happened upon *Clash* late one night on TV. It blew my mind.

The hero of *Clash* is Perseus, played by the impossibly beautiful Harry Hamlin, a sweetly dumb fantasy jock – all tanned muscles and pudding-bowl curls in a nip-slip toga. He hears of a princess, Andromeda (played by Judi Bowker), who lives under a curse placed upon her by her spurned ex Calibos, the highly problematic son of sea goddess Thetis, and he soon pledges to save Andromeda. Calibos has recently been cursed himself, transformed by Zeus into a hideous (but ripped) satyr-like creature, and Andromeda can barely look at him. And so he creates an unwinnable contest for her suitors: a tricky riddle that must be answered correctly on pain of death – and any number of clueless princes have already met a grisly end.

As the secret son of Zeus, Perseus is favoured by the gods; but all is not well on Mount Olympus and Thetis works behind the scenes so that Calibos might prevail and marry Andromeda himself. Of course, Perseus – using gifts from the gods – solves the riddle and he and Andromeda are soon hitched, but that's where things get spicy.

At the wedding, Andromeda's mother claims that her daughter is 'even more lovely than the goddess Thetis herself' and the great sea goddess (in a marvellously camp performance from Maggie Smith) is pissed. Her own colossal monument suddenly crumbles and her pale marble head rolls terrifyingly through the crowd. When it springs to life – something that freaked me out as a child – Thetis finally speaks. She demands that Andromeda be sacrificed to the Kraken, an incredibly swole sea monster. Perseus has just 30 days to complete a dangerous quest to obtain a super-weapon to save her: the head of Medusa. With its young, handsome and nearly naked hero (Perseus), its camp evil queen (Thetis), fey flying horse (Pegasus) and all manner of magic and monsters, *Clash* had me spellbound. Perseus became my personal hero, although I sometimes wondered: did I want to be him, or be *with* him?

From that first fateful viewing, I read every myth and legend I could, from Roger Lancelyn Green's *Tales of the Greek Heroes* (1958), illustrated by the iconic Pauline Baynes (favoured artist of J R R Tolkien and C S Lewis), to Edith Hamilton's *Mythology* (1942) and even Usborne's *Supernatural Guides* and *World of the Unknown* series, but I could find none of the queer magic I was seeking. As a teenager, I discovered the (accidentally) homoerotic sci-fi fantasy artwork of Mark Harrison and Frank Frazetta, with their muscular heroes and oily barbarians, all bulging boobs and codpieces, phallic magical swords and thick-thighed centaurs. But, as raunchy as it all was, it was gay in subtext only.

I watched *Clash* again and again and again over the years, but as I grew older and, I guess, even queerer, something changed in how I viewed it. Just as Perseus had once glowed, Calibos now simmered. While Andromeda had previously sparkled on the screen, Medusa – all scales and fury – took her place in my mind as *Clash*'s truly wronged woman. Both Calibos and Medusa, misunderstood by society, are abused and ostracized;

and, although they choose darkness instead of turning towards the light, they seemed pretty queer to me. It made me wonder if there might be more queerness glittering inside the stories of old, hidden from view, and I set out to unearth it.

You will not find Calibos and Medusa in these pages; sadly, they are just too villainous to be celebrated as heroes. But they are the creatures who sent me on my own quest to discover the true queer stars of myth and legend: the gay, lesbian and bisexual role models, the gender-nonconforming love (and hate) stories, and the powerful trans and nonbinary archetypes that appear again and again throughout the ancient stories. Hidden in the margins of history books, classical literature and thousands of years of heroic tales, there is a diverse, otherworldly super-community of queer heroes to discover, learn from and celebrate.

But, like any hero's quest, there are pitfalls in digging around in the past for queerness. The gates are guarded by pearl-clutching academics and Victorian-spirited scholars who have traditionally winced at the idea of ancient queer love. We must also navigate some tired tropes, from Bury Your Gays, where queer characters are more expendable than straight ones, and Lesbian Tragedy, which decrees that if two women fall in love then at least one of them must die. It should also be acknowledged that contemporary notions of sexuality, gender identity and queerness are, well, contemporary, and do not always fit neatly over stories from ancient times. But, while not everything can be queer-edged, there is often a gay glimmer that has been ignored, mocked or suppressed by those in the know.

Meet Patroclus and Achilles (explored in Madeline Miller's bestseller *The Song of Achilles*) and the sprawling queer Greek pantheon. Revisit Sappho, queen of the lesbians, and get to know pot-smoking Amazons, protective Vodou deities, Norse tricksters, the *Mahābhārata*'s genderqueer Shikhandi, and the stars of a bisexual Arthurian three-way.

Because of *Clash*, and my love of 1980s, 1990s and end-of-millennium pop culture and activist groups, I have also been a little flexible in my approach (and why not?). Meet too the Order of Chaeronea, a secret queer cabal of elites from the time of Oscar Wilde; the Minoan Brotherhood, a gay male-witch community born out of the post-Stonewall summer of gay power; and Daughters of Bilitis, a lesbian activist group who loved to dance. And alongside texts like Shakespeare's *Twelfth Night* are clever contemporary spins of the tales of old, from literary characters like Virginia Woolf's Orlando and Maurice Sendak's Wild Things, to Anne Rice's 'first vampire same-sex parents' Lestat and Louis, and even gaymer deity Zelda. Meet comic stars like Neil Gaiman's Dream, aka the Sandman, plus mythical Marvel characters and legendary TV personas from *Doctor Who*, *Xena: Warrior Princess* and *Buffy the Vampire Slayer*.

There is much wisdom to learn from these timeless heroes who have commanded armies, fallen in and out of love, placed curses on gender boundaries and fought to be themselves. But, if there's one thing I hope you take from this book it is that being a gay demigod, lesbian Valkyrie, trans literary creation, eight-legged flying horse, bisexual Knight of the Round Table, or teenage witch with 1990s mall-Goth styling is no barrier to greatness: we can (all) be heroes.

Some notes on the use of 'LGBTQ+' and 'queer' in *Queer Heroes of Myth and Legend*

In this book, I use the term 'LGBTQ+'. It's an initialism in flux, with different communities and individuals using it in clever, creative and subjective ways. The + sign does a lot of heroic lifting: it encompasses a multitude of both fixed and shifting identities and intersections that don't fit neatly into lesbian, gay, bisexual or trans categories. Why? Well, I wanted to include everybody, from gay gods and sapphic saints to gender-nonconforming djinn.

'Queer' is a catch-all for some, bringing together LGBTQ+ people into one sprawling family; for others, queer is an identity itself. It's also an academic movement with a retro 1990s edge that seeks a new way of analysing a culture built around straight expectations, all to a Spice Girls soundtrack. Some might point out that queer was once a slur – and even though it is now widely thought to have been reclaimed, not all agree. What this shows, to me at least, is that both queer and LGBTQ+ are terms that imply huge diversity of thought and interpretation. And so, in these pages, queer relies on context. It will almost always be shorthand for 'gay' or 'lesbian' or 'trans', but it might sometimes point to something that, well, just isn't 'straight'. Oh, and one last thing: queer is a noun but also sometimes a verb. Confused? You'll get it, I know you will.

ACHILLES AND PATROCLUS

The godly golden frat boy and his mortal geek boyfriend

Achilles is the achingly beautiful demigod of Ancient Greece, desperate to realize his destiny as a legendary war hero. At his side is Patroclus, his complicated, mortal companion, advisor and lover. Although somewhat side-players in the wider story of the Trojan War, the pair's relationship shines out from the classics, from Homer's *Iliad* to the works of Aeschylus and Plato. Its queerness was hidden in the margins of history until classics teacher and author Madeline Miller deftly refocused the myth, bringing this tragic, musclebound love story to the fore.

In her award-winning and bestselling novel *The Song of Achilles* (2011), Miller deals with the Achilles and Patroclus of the *Iliad*, drawing on the original, master-tape narrative of their incredible relationship. Although Miller didn't set out to write an explicitly 'gay' love story, the sense of 'physical

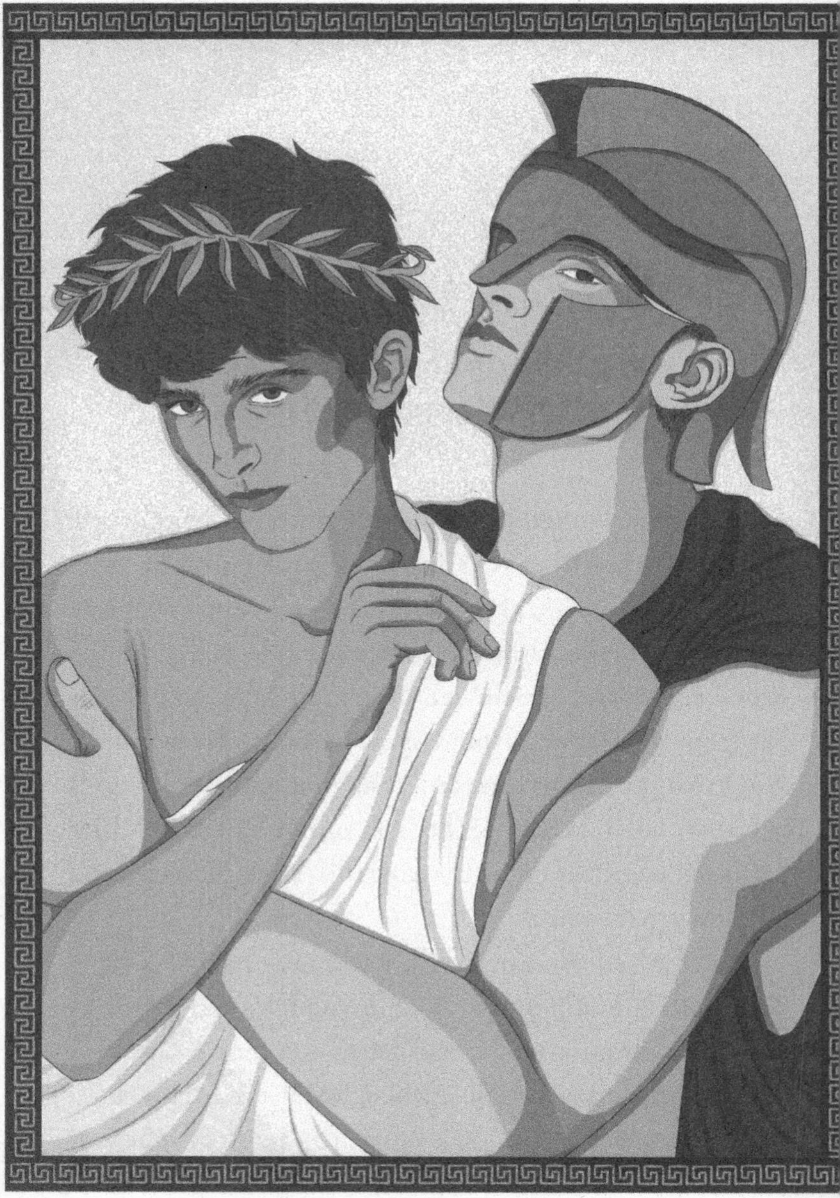

devastation' that Achilles feels on the death of Patroclus spoke deeply to her; put simply, there was no way to see these characters other than as two men in love.

Miller decodes what she sees as the central mystery of the *Iliad*: that of the turnaround of Achilles' seemingly unshakable stubbornness to continue to fight in what has become a senseless, blighted war. In Shakespeare's *Troilus and Cressida* (1609), the same scene plays out rather queerly indeed: the Greek commanders cannot even with Achilles, who refuses to come out and fight, suggesting that it is his time in a tent with Patroclus 'upon a lazy bed the livelong day' that has made him so 'dainty of his worth'. In all the stories, Achilles has become immovable – until, that is, he hears Patroclus has been killed.

In the *Iliad*, it is how Achilles reacts to Patroclus's death – a scene of high drama – that underlines their love. Achilles refuses to fight to protect his honour, and Patroclus (in a near-magical trance, in Miller's novel) ultimately dresses up in Achilles' armour and heads out onto the battlefield. Although he fights with the singular force of a man desperately in love, he has just a fraction of Achilles' own fighting power and is eventually killed. Hector, Prince of Troy, thinks he is Achilles and brutally slays him. Overcome with grief, Achilles' sole focus is to avenge his lover's death; his feat of frenzied bloodlust ultimately ends his own life, earning him a place in legend.

Miller's take is at odds with that of certain historians, some of whom wince at the idea of Achilles and Patroclus in love, but her source material suggests otherwise. In Book 18 of the *Iliad*, Achilles claims that he loved Patroclus as his own life; and in another section, the dying Achilles asks for them to be buried together – something Miller plays on in *Song*, helping push the pair back into contemporary queer consciousness. Their constant struggle to have their unique bond recognized, in both familial and political spheres, is certainly a queer experience the author seeks to highlight. But Miller has fun too. We all know of couples where one basks in the golden light of fame while the other sits around grumpily tending to their lover's whims. But the author plays with specifically queer iconography, making the lives of these two mythical men seem, well, pretty *gay*.

There's also the glittering, pink-crystal-lined cave of Chiron, the burly centaur and educator who looms large in the lives of Achilles and Patroclus like some hot gay zaddy. It's not just Miller who finds fascination here: there are endless classical paintings depicting a nubile but nervous Achilles and the thick-thighed, lusty Chiron weighing down on him (the man was half-horse, after all). There are also the allusions to sex and muscle-worship, to Achilles' physical perfection and frat-boy persona, and to geeky Patroclus's unrequited love, the queerest trope of all.

DIONYSUS

The Greek pantheon's Pét Nat-loving bisexual party king

As the god of wine and fertility, Dionysus is the Greek pantheon's party king, the conjurer of orgiastic rites and ritual and a longhaired stoner who sways tipsily through the mythical texts in skimpy goatskin briefs, a bottomless cup of wine in hand. He would transform himself or his followers into animals or multiple versions of himself, drive others to madness, and would often appear with the tempting offer of a honey-dipped fennel stalk. But beyond the hedonism is a complex main character, a queer hero who balanced the godlike figure he was expected to be with the messy, earthly being he truly was.

Dionysus had rather queer beginnings. He is said to have been born twice: once by his mortal mother (and saved at the point of her sudden death, Harry Potter-style), before being sewn into Zeus's thigh until he reached maturity and was born again, a god. The idea of this second birth gave Dionysus instant mystery-cult status and he was worshipped in secretive ancient communities until the early Christians trademarked being born again. His second birth from a man's body places Dionysus in a more contemporary space – one where gender is unset and exists in a more malleable, slippery state. He was also raised as a girl, a disguise to protect him from Zeus's much-maligned yet long-suffering wife, Hera; and although early depictions of Dionysus are of a bearded man, in post-classical art he was transformed into a sinuous femme-presenting boy, a sort of gender-nonconforming club kid for the ancient age.

As an adult, Dionysus was bisexual, falling in love with both men and women. Although he married Ariadne, he originally rolled around with Ampelos, a young and handsome satyr. In Book 3 of Roman poet Ovid's *Fasti* (1st century BCE), Ampelos is described as the son of a nymph and a satyr who was loved by Dionysus and died on a dare to pick grapes from a tree. And in Nonnus's *Dionysiaca* (5th century CE), Ampelos is gored by a bull and his blood creates the first grapevine. Brokenhearted, Dionysus lifts him up into the stars to become the grape-gatherer constellation. It's the fantastical gay-tragedy trope that launched a thousand fanfic pages.

His indefinable gender and sexuality and party-monster status made Dionysus a touchstone in ancient and post-classical art. His stories are explored like hot gossip through Athenian vases in the mid-6th century, and through sarcophagi and countless Renaissance paintings and sculptures, revealing lurid parties in the woods with near-naked devotees and more hard-ons than you can shake a fennel stem at. In the eyes of the artists most tantalized by Dionysus, the god's gatherings would be boozy, animalistic affairs. He is usually flanked by the maenads, his band of female ravers, and the satyrs, impossibly beautiful young men with horses' ears and everlasting erections. There's a full-blooded ultra-hedonism that powers the myth of Dionysus, celebrating life, physical pleasure, ecstasy and identity. To many, he's the god of not giving AF.

But the figure of Dionysus also served to forewarn, to show what might happen if morals were forgotten, lines blurred, robes dropped and the excesses of human nature left unbridled. In ancient times, failure to worship him might summon him to your village, turning the women into maenads who might rip the local men to shreds in fits of rapture. It is perhaps this sticky relationship between ecstasy and destruction that continues to fascinate and inspire.

Donna Tartt's barnstorming novel *The Secret History* (1992) explores the deathly effects of the recreation of Dionysian ritual among a group of privileged students at a private school, and he is referenced in popular culture from *Xena: Warrior Princess* and *Riverdale* to avant-garde film like

Brian De Palma's early experimental doc *Dionysus in '69*, where a theatre troupe writhes around in jockstraps. The legendary parties of the 1970s gay-liberation era had a Dionysian spirit; and today the slow creep of ayahuasca ceremonies and micro-dosing into modern hipster circles feels in sync with this transformative being.

Perhaps the queerest, most complicated hero in the Greek pantheon, Dionysus is many things all at once, an almost indefinable being who simply loves to party. Although the idea that queer love might happen only as a byproduct of ultra-hedonism is problematic to say the least, let's think of Big D as a liberator. He frees men, women and everyone in between of their inhibitions, their hetero- or homonormativity, if only for one Pét Nat-fuelled, gender-bending night under the stars.

PAN

The hairy-legged goat-daddy of the eternal cruising grounds

The fuzziest god of the Greek pantheon, Pan is lord of the wild, lusty shepherds, budding fertility and impromptus (improv music and theatre – but don't hold that against him). As the goat-man wandered Arcadia, the densely wooded heart of the Peloponnese, it became the ultimate queer cruising ground. Imagine the sweet, soft rustle of the undergrowth, the crunch of twigs and leaves under hoof, breathy notes from a set of panpipes and then the hurried grunts of a hairy-legged man getting off: this was Pan's domain.

Although youthful in spirit, Pan is ancient. In mythical terms, he is older than even the Olympians, making his origin story rather murky, although similar elemental nature spirits appear in many cultures. He has the thick legs of a goat, a clunky set of hooves, a man's top half (albeit with a pair of shiny horns) and an insatiable urge to play music, jack his beanstalk, and nap.

The god of creative fervour, physical energy and siesta, Pan is naturally thought of as the god of sex and sexuality too. He took a male lover, a Sicilian shepherd named Daphnis who created pastoral poetry (and met an untimely end at the hands of a jealous nymph). A 1st-century Roman marble sculpture (after a Greek original) at the National Archaeological Museum of Naples shows Pan and Daphnis together, with Daphnis trying to play a set of pipes and Pan yawn-reaching his arm around him in an overbearing fashion.

In ancient times, Pan inspired a sort of rustic worship, with shrines and statues rather than temples, but it was in the late 19th century that he truly made his mark on contemporary culture. In the late 1890s, Western society was Pan-crazy. While *Dracula*, *Frankenstein* and *The Strange Case of Dr Jekyll and Mr Hyde* explore the monsters that lurk within all men, academic Victor Imko points out this Victorian Pan reboot coincided with the emergence of gay male identity. In an essay published in the journal *Chrestomathy* (vol. 12, 2013), Imko nods to several works, including Arthur Machen's Victorian horror story *The Great God Pan* (1894), about an outbreak of gay panic in easily scandalized Victorian London, and E F Benson's Pan-powered 'The Man Who Went Too Far' (1904), which showed the awful things that would happen should queerness be allowed to flourish.

On the sidelines, occultist Aleister Crowley (a sort of real-life *Doctor Who* steampunk villain) led a ritual known as the Night of Pan, where Crowley's followers would slip into a trance in the horny god's name. But, for everyone else, Pan meant psychic trouble. It's easy to see how this half-man, half-goat became the embodiment of duality, the human versus the untamed animal nature the Victorians so feared. That some might hide a sort of queerness within became a terrifying, panic-inducing idea. In fact, the word 'panic' derives from Pan himself.

It must have been hard for Victorians to ignore the eye-poppingly graphic depictions of Pan left over from ancient times – statues with gigantic phalluses, or depictions of Pan getting hot and heavy with a goat. For the Victorians, this freewheeling, animalistic god embodied a fear of sexuality, with Pan signifying queerness itself. But this god of the wild was ultimately acting on his most innate urges: does this mean his endless gay romping in the woods could only have been, well, kind of natural? The Victorians struggled to explain it, and instead emphasized the cloven feet and goat horns that lent Pan a certain satanic edge.

Pan continues to clop through pop culture, from the truly odd comedy-fantasy movie *7 Faces of Dr Lao* (1964) where he seduces Barbara Eden with his set of pipes, to Tim Curry's horned god, Darkness, in Ridley Scott's fan-favourite *Legend*

(1985), and Guillermo del Toro's *Pan's Labyrinth* (2006). But the most faithful, queer-edged depiction of Pan is in Armistead Maupin's cult-classic novel *Tales of the City* (1978), in which Michael Tolliver, a man who has escaped the Bible Belt with its oppressive Victorian values, finds true gay liberation in San Francisco.

One Halloween, he dresses as the one character that can embody this new freedom: Pan. 'His horns were outrageously realistic,' writes Maupin. 'His mock-chinchilla Home Yardage goat haunches jutted out from his waist with comic eroticism. His belly was flat, and his pecs . . . well, his pecs were the pecs of a man who hardly ever cheated on a bench press at the Y [the 1978 version of never missing a leg day].' If the Victorians feared the way that Pan connects us to our animalistic nature, by the era of *Tales of the City*, this queer thread to our inner, 'true' self is to be celebrated, not suppressed. As Michael readies himself before leaving the house, Maupin writes: 'Pan is on the rampage tonight!'

THE AMAZONS

The musclebound, pot-smoking wonder women of the ancient world

The Amazons are the mythical warrior women of the ancient world, musclebound matriarchs who matched – and often bettered – men in strength, physical prowess, hunting and combat. They had little use for men, who were used merely to procreate, and preferred their own company. They also loved tattoos, wearing comfortable trousers and, according to Herodotus, smoked a lot of pot. So far, so butch.

In the oldest mythical texts, the Amazons are rarely revered. In fact, they serve as a warning: ancient male scholars saw these manless women as near-monstrous, cruel murderesses and slayers of men (almost every hero in the Greek pantheon has a brush with the Amazons). To later scholars, the idea of a society of women without men, hunting and protecting their travelling nation, was preposterous and some feared that the Amazons were – whisper it – *lesbian*, at least symbolically.

Not every male scholar has found the warrior-woman archetype so frightening. In 1941, a radical and privately polyamorous throuple the Marston-Byrnes used Amazonian mythology as a creative response to what they thought was a growing social problem. William Marston, a psychologist, inventor and writer, noted a growing disillusionment with gender conformity, particularly among young women. The Marston-Byrnes' remedy was nothing less than extraordinary: they created Wonder Woman. William saw the huge educational potential of comics and collaborated with attorney and psychologist Elizabeth Holloway Marston (his wife) and Olive Byrne (the Marston's third partner), an accomplished psychology researcher, to conjure a new type of superhero; someone less smash-'em-up and more powered by ideals of love. 'Fine,' said Elizabeth (according to Boston University alumna Marguerite Lamb). 'But make her a woman.'

Wonder Woman, aka Diana Prince, was everything an Amazonian superhero should be: strong, wise, powerful and benevolent. She was a superpowered being from the Amazon Isles, sculpted from clay and given life by her mother, Queen Hippolyta, before taking on the mantle of protector of the 'Man's World'. In this new version of the Amazon legend, which debuted in *Sensation Comics* #1, January 1942, the Marston-Byrnes created a tough-ass matriarchal super-race – technologically advanced and battle-ready but abhorring war. 'Wonder Woman is psychological propaganda for the new type of woman who should, I believe, rule the world,' said William. 'Not even girls want to be girls so long as our feminine archetype lacks force, strength and power.'

Everything about the Marston-Byrnes was unique. Elizabeth was the breadwinner, Byrne was the birth mother to two of the family's four children, and William was an avowed feminist. Byrne and the Marstons took part in an unorthodox marriage ceremony after which Byrne wore a thick bangle on each arm rather than a ring, much like Wonder Woman herself. In fact, it is Byrne who is thought to have been the real inspiration behind the character.

In recent times, this Amazonian myth has become less fantastical and, – thrillingly – much more evidential. Archaeologists and historians are connecting disparate discoveries that challenge how gendered our perception of ancient societies has been. The Amazons of ancient times had most in common with the Scythians, an ancient horseriding people living in small tribes throughout ancient Eurasia; micro societies where women lived, worked, rode horses and hunted alongside men. In 2019, archaeologists discovered the remains of four female warriors buried with a battery of arrowheads, spears and horse tack in a tomb in western Russia – exactly where Ancient Greek stories placed their Amazonian legends. And there have been other Scythian discoveries: frozen bodies with tattooed skin, tattoo kits, evidence of cannabis-smoking, and the dregs of a powerful mare's-milk moonshine.

For some, the tattooed, weed-smoking, big-bicep Amazons of myth are a truly horrifying concept, and for others, this gender-nonconforming Amazonian world is a butch lesbian utopia (if the Amazons aren't gay, then they certainly aren't straight). Without rewriting history, but rather refocusing on it, we can see that warrior women – leaders of nations, hunters and fighters – aren't just a heteronormative fairy tale; they have existed for aeons. These are the Amazons of fact, the warrior women who inspired the Ancient Greek stories and who have struck fear in the hearts of men, and joy in the hearts of women, ever since.

NARCISSUS

The tragic, non-heteronormative heartthrob of self-care

There is a trippy, bejewelled fever dream of a film that has been hugely influential on queer art. It is *Pink Narcissus* (1971), James Bidgood's experimental, DIY masterpiece that follows the homoerotic daydreams of a young male beauty lounging in his kitsch apartment among wafting drapes, satin sheets and countless gilded mirrors that help conjure his narcissistic reveries. Its fantastical, gaudy, bare-bum aesthetic is evident in the work of photographers Pierre et Gilles and David LaChapelle, and even in Baz Luhrmann's queer-toned films. And at its core is the myth of Narcissus, an ancient and tragic warning tale of the dangers of self-obsession, but one that also deals with male beauty and man-on-man desire. The Narcissus myth, with all its remixing and retelling, has become a core tenet of queer cultural expression: he was a man who refused to live up to heteronormative expectations and paid a heavy price.

In ancient myth, Narcissus was the son of either the river god Cephissus and the nymph Liriope, or the moon goddess Selene and her mortal man-crush Endymion. But in both versions of the story, one thing is clear: Narcissus grows up to be a total stunner. And Ovid's epic *Metamorphoses* tells the story of how Narcissus's beauty becomes his downfall.

When Narcissus was born, his mother consulted a seer who predicted a long, wonderful life for the newborn, but only if he never discovered himself. When the nymph Echo saw the adult Narcissus strolling through the forest, she fell in love with him immediately – but he rejected her. Such was the extent of her heartbreak that she wandered the woods until she faded away and was no more than an echo of her voice. The goddess Nemesis, an aspect of Aphrodite, decided to punish Narcissus for spurning the nymph, and led him to a silvery pool of thirst-quenching water. On seeing his reflection, perhaps for the first time in his life, Narcissus fell deeply and passionately in love. As he slowly realized how futile his situation was, he transformed into a small white-and-gold flower.

The Narcissus of myth rejects marriage and the family pressures to take a wife and then meets a tragic end. Rightly so, according to Ovid, whose early version of the story focuses on Narcissus's heartbroken, grumpy admirers as victims of his self-obsession. But, by medieval times, his story has evolved to one of surprising modernity: Narcissus is seen instead as a failed lover who struggled to have empathy with others. He simply doesn't love women the way he should and exists outside of the heteronormative world with all its pressures of marriage and baby-making. Which is, you know, pretty queer. Most importantly, it is not just his own reflection that Narcissus falls in love with, but the image of a man.

The tragic story has enthralled artists, poets and writers for centuries, from Ovid to Keats and Caravaggio to Dalí, and Narcissus's tale has haunted our understanding of psychoanalysis, ego and personality. It's almost impossible to view the Narcissus myth without its queer coding, but the story has also muddied the waters of understanding same-sex love. Narcissus's end suggests there is something antisocial, self-absorbed and amoral about his desire, and this take on gayness has somewhat endured in popular thought.

In 2004, Dr Benjamin Henry at Oxford University discovered an earlier, much queerer version of the Narcissus myth, one that sees him spurn several male lovers, including Ameinias, to whom he gives a sword and who eventually dies by suicide – the same fate accorded to Narcissus, who cannot live without the object of his desire. Little has changed with the mechanics of the story, but its queer edge is now undeniable.

In *Pink Narcissus*, the dreamy, visionary moments of the
protagonist's fantasies as he rummages around in his undies
contrast with the harsh reality of his life as a sex worker.
Between the grimy moments looking for trade, his make-
believe world cannot truly sustain him. Perhaps this is the true
theme of the Narcissus myth: the damaging effect of being
forced to hide one's true self from the world and losing yourself
to fantasy.

POSEIDON AND PELOPS

The legendary sea-zaddy power top and his young male lover

The ancient god of the ocean, earthquakes and horses, Poseidon is the slippery-when-wet, trident-bearing superbeing, and the fractious brother of Zeus and Hades. In classical art, epic poems and countless fountains across the world, his thick thighs, rippling muscles, full, flowing beard and long locks give him real sea-zaddy energy. Worshipped across the ancient world as one of the most powerful gods, second only to Zeus, he was particularly loved in Athens and Corinth and feared everywhere else; he was tempestuous, heavy-handed, and hilariously thin-skinned, flinging deathly tidal waves at anyone who looked at him sideways. He is best known for ruining things – the battle for Troy, the hero Odysseus's long journey home – and for having a brood of truly monstrous children, including Antaeus the giant, Charybdis the overly dramatic sea creature, and Arion, a small talking horse.

Perhaps Poseidon avoided talking about his offspring with Pelops, his male lover who is celebrated as the inspiration behind the Olympic Games in the tales of old, even though their relationship has often been politely pushed into the margins. Like Poseidon, Pelops became a celebrity in his own right. Having won the crown of the Greek city of Pisa, he was the ruler of western Peloponnesus, that is, the Island of Pelops, and he also survived one of the most gruesome incidents of ancient times.

In a bid to test the carelessness of the gods, Pelops's father, King Tantalus, tried to trick them into eating something that should never have been on the menu. Throwing a banquet, he killed and butchered Pelops then boiled him and served him up to the Olympians. Zeus saw the deception immediately, cast Tantalus into the depths of Tartarus and set about reassembling Pelops and bringing him back to life (less his shoulder, which had been accidentally eaten by a hungry Demeter). It was after this resurrection that Poseidon showed interest in the young man and took him to Mount Olympus as an apprentice.

But what of the pair's time on Olympus? How did they spend their days? Whatever happened on that mountain, feverish fanfic authors have done well in imagining it. And in his cult book *Lovers' Legends: The Gay Greek Myths* (2002), Andrew Calimach has his own learned version of their relationship:

'The first god ever to love a man was Poseidon, who loved Pelops,' he writes. Calimach sheds light on the goings-on between Poseidon and Pelops, imagining the moment the great sea-zaddy set eyes on Pelops, freshly resurrected: 'all his homeliness had boiled away, and his beauty glowed from every pore. Poseidon sat riveted, lost in wonder.' In Calimach's version, drawing on the ancient works of 5th-century BCE poets like Pindar, the pair fly away on Poseidon's chariot pulled by golden horses and are soon shacked up in Zeus's palace. 'He settled in with Pelops as lover and beloved . . . Pelops loved the great bearded god and hung on his every word.' As Pindar himself wrote, Poseidon's heart was 'mad with desire', with Pelops 'stirring Poseidon's love'.

This romantic side of Poseidon has seldom been explored in popular culture. The Poseidon of literature and film is either a statesmanlike elder, a superhero with toga and trident, or an amorphous ocean disturbance. In *Clash of the Titans* (1981), Poseidon appears silently under the sea, teasing out his sea monster. Although perfectly played by Jack Gwillim (King Aeetes in *Jason and the Argonauts*, 1963), he is frail, like a character in old-timers-versus-aliens movie *Cocoon* (1985). Other moviemakers have more fun with Poseidon. The 2011 film *Immortals* (2011) is delightfully queer-coded, with glittering gold battle-drag, shirtless hunks with flawless skin, and grumpy musings in clipped accents giving Mount Olympus the feel of a posh school for bisexuals. In *Immortals*, Poseidon is a young, musclebound heartthrob with a sassy shell-like crown and is prone to tempestuous rages. Something about this accidentally homoerotic adaptation feels close to the original, Ancient Greek version of Poseidon, even though the great sea god's interest in the male form is only subtly coded and not explicitly explored. If most literary and cinematic versions of Poseidon overlook his lust for men, he remains as unpredictable and untamed as ever. The great god of the sea is less a hot mess than a glistening wet one.

ARTEMIS

The woodsy hunting goddess with Big Dyke Energy

Artemis, the ancient goddess with undeniable Big Dyke Energy, has been thought of as lesbian, or at least lesbian-adjacent, for centuries. In recent years, queer scholars have wandered the archives, dusting off ancient tomes and revisiting the Sapphic records, seeking hard evidence to bring her officially into the LGBTQ+ family. But was Artemis a lesbian in vibe only? Let's look for the clues to explain the woodsy hunting goddess's jaw-dropping BDE.

Artemis is the goddess of the hunt, the wild and vegetation, but she is also the deity assigned to oversee the Herculean acts of childbirth and childcare, the protector of young women and girls, and is often linked to the moon and the sacred feminine. The ancient scholars all agree that she is handsome, healthy, tall and immensely strong. Due to her hunting prowess, she is known as 'she who delights in arrows' and is, of course, a dog

lover. Thought to be linked to a Neolithic bear cult and its accompanying deities, she was thought of by the Ancient Greeks as one singular brute force. Her pledge to remain forever unmarried gave her even more power, as she is one of the few gods Aphrodite, the goddess of love, cannot control. In all mythical stories surrounding Artemis, it is her tough personality that shines through; she is one to be reckoned with. A power top rather than a bossy bottom.

But the queerest thing about Artemis is her avowed avoidance of marriage. She is often referred to as the maiden or virgin goddess, but the meaning of the word 'virgin' in the ancient texts is interchangeable with 'unmarried'. Could this be code for 'lesbian'? After all, Artemis merely wants to enjoy the company of women and live her own life running free and nude in the forest, being the very best at competitive sports – and to gruesomely murder any man who slights her or sees her naked.

When a young man, Actaeon, happens upon Artemis skinny-dipping in a pond in the woods, she transforms him into a deer and watches as he is savagely attacked and eaten by his own hunting dogs. When another man, Buphagus, even *thinks* about Artemis in the nude, she reads his mind and strikes him down; and when Broteas refuses to honour her, she makes him crazy, so he walks into a fire, dying in agony. There are just three men who have positive interactions with Artemis: one is her twin brother, Apollo; another is Orion, her beloved hunting buddy (making Orion the pantheon's official lez-bro); and the third is Daphnis, the twinky male lover of Dionysus who served to entertain her with his panpipes.

Artemis's role in the problematic Callisto myth is the most obvious purple flag marking out the goddess as gay. Callisto is one of Artemis's hunting attendants and has a special role in Artemis's entourage of semi-naked nymphs and assorted gal pals. King of the gods Zeus, in all his chauvinistic and supremely creepy power, decides to seduce Callisto. Knowing that the young beauty has taken Artemis's no-men-allowed oath, he attempts to deceive her, appearing in disguise. Taking other, unexpected forms, from animals to showers of gold, was Zeus's favourite way to violate women; only, but with Callisto, he is forced to take the one form she most trusts – that of Artemis herself.

The idea that Artemis was the true object of Callisto's desire rings lesbian alarm bells across the ancient texts and it also placed the goddess in the sights of the great painters, almost all men, who appear to have been titillated by the idea of Sapphic love. Depictions of Artemis take on an erotic feel, but this version of Artemis serves only to satisfy the hetero male gaze, much like Actaeon's peeping-tomfoolery as he gazes upon the naked goddess during her self-care ritual.

In the end, Artemis and Callisto's relationship sours. After Zeus's visit, the pair are skinny-dipping and Artemis sees that Callisto is pregnant. Furious, she turns Callisto into a bear who, according to all versions of the myth, is eventually placed in the heavens for her safety. The moral of the story (if there is one) is unclear, but it is a man who comes between Artemis and Callisto. The young woman's fate is sealed, the goddess enacts her revenge and Callisto is no more. Unfortunately, that's how it goes with the Lesbian Tragedy trope.

From the ancient epic poems to her crumbled temple in Ephesus, Turkey, through to classical art, Artemis has retained her power over the pantheon. To the men who have written about her, built monuments to her, or painted her likeness, she is unpredictable, short-tempered trouble, or simply an erotic creation to secretly perve over. But all their stories, sculpture and art seem forced to acknowledge Artemis as an extremely self-possessed spirit with feminist ideals and a natural affinity and protective urge towards other women. Perhaps there is no need to bring Artemis into the queer family; she has always been there.

ANTINOUS

Lord of leg day, lover of a Roman emperor, and cultish gay deity

God of swole, lord of leg day and unofficial patron saint of six-packs, Antinous has one shapely foot firmly planted in myth and the other in historical reality, with the sizzling gay passion of his onetime lover, Roman emperor Hadrian, nestled in between. This handsome, musclebound celebrity youth was once known across the empire; after he tragically drowned, he transformed into something else entirely. What followed were countless shirtless statues and erotic artworks with Antinous '. . . immortalized so uniquely and so profusely in marble', according to historian Royston Lambert in *Beloved and God: The Story of Hadrian and Antinous* (1984). Then came temples, shrines and other magnificent erections; Antinous was ultimately deified by a heartbroken Roman emperor, transforming from toned and terrific to melancholy and mythic.

The real, pre-deity Antinous was born around 111 CE in Claudiopolis, Greece (now Turkey). Little is known about his life before meeting Hadrian, who arrived in Antinous's hometown in 123 CE. Although young Antinous was soon despatched to study in Italy, the pair reunited there some time later. They loved to hunt together, and evidence suggests Hadrian found Antinous wise beyond his years. By 128 CE the young, handsome and athletic Claudiopolitan had found his way into Hadrian's heart to become the emperor's favourite.

The role of the favourite is unique; it can be that of glorified servant to the ruling monarch, confidant, yes-man and best friend – but also sometimes his bedfellow. Though held in high regard, the favourite occupies a position that is always precarious: they might 'have the ear' of their master, exerting subtle power and influence, but they could also lose their status on a whim, forfeiting everything – possibly even their life. Some historians have suggested a coercive relationship here, and Hadrian's obvious closeness to Antinous did cause something of a stir in elite circles. After all, the emperor had a wife, Sabina. But same-sex favourites and bisexuality were somewhat acceptable in the upper echelons of society, and Hadrian and Antinous were indeed inseparable.

Hadrian liked to explore his sprawling empire, overseeing its farthest reaches and nipping any potential resistance in the bud. And so, with the long-suffering Sabina in tow, Hadrian and Antinous embarked on an empire-wide tour, from Syria to Judea (where he contentiously built a temple to Zeus on the site of a Jewish temple). But tongues had started to wag, and the men were soon the subject of gossip.

They arrived in Egypt to hunt down a lion near Alexandria; in the aftermath, Hadrian commissioned monuments, poems and writings depicting himself bravely saving Antinous from the jaws of the lion itself. After the pomp and fizz of his press campaign, Hadrian continued to live as if he were inside his own mythical story, with Antinous by his side. He organized a flotilla of Roman senior officers, scholars and celebs to travel up the Nile, but somewhere near the temple of Thoth, and around the time of the festival of Osiris, Antinous mysteriously drowned.

Although Royston Lambert's book is a factual retelling of the relationship between Hadrian and Antinous, it sometimes reads like an Agatha Christie novel – see how in 'the slanting sunlight' a body was found in the 'murky, receding waters of the river Nile. It was that of a young man, athletic in build, with a massive chest, hair clustered over the brow and down the neck in thick curls and a broad face of such unusual and poignant beauty that it was to haunt the imagination and conscience of civilized men for nearly two thousand years.' Historians are undecided on whodunnit. A jealous courtier?

Agents of Sabina? Was it an accident, death by suicide, or was it Hadrian himself?

The emperor found himself caught in a swell of intense grief. He halted his tour for a year and set about commemorating Antinous's life – which he would not do quietly. Hadrian commissioned a city to be built in Antinous's honour, named a star and lotus flower after him, and took the extraordinary step of declaring him a deity, an act reserved only for the emperor and his family. Ultimately, Hadrian created a cult around Antinous, which over the years flourished across the empire; there is archaeological evidence of public and private worship, and more than 28 temples to Hadrian's lost love.

Today, finally, there is realistic scholarly discussion surrounding Hadrian and Antinous's relationship, but throughout the centuries there has been much historical hand-wringing about the fact that they were a couple. In the past, ancient artifacts that speak of Antinous's beauty and firm pecs, or that underline gay love, have proved to be uncomfortable finds and, as Lambert writes, '. . . studies of Hadrian either ignore altogether or skate gingerly around the issue of his . . . homosexuality or bisexuality'. It will take time for historians to unpick the true story of Hadrian and Antinous, but – thanks to a wealth of evidence – there is one thing we know for sure: theirs is a tale of two men in love.

SAPPHO

The ancient erotic poet and lesbian Lin-Manuel Miranda

The life and work of bisexual Greek poet Sappho of Lesbos, official Queen of the Lesbians, forms part of the foundations of contemporary queer culture. Born in the 7th century BCE, Sappho is one of the world's most lauded writers and a true celesbian of the ancient era. Plato called her the 'Tenth Muse', she has inspired countless other writers and academics for thousands of years, and she even inspired the words we use to describe desire between women. She wrote honestly and passionately about love and jealousy and the joy and pain of everyday life.

Born to a wealthy family, Sappho is thought to have run an academy for young women until she became famous for her poetry. She was a lyric poet, writing words to be sung, making her a sort of lesbian Lin-Manuel Miranda of ancient times. As tastes changed, Sappho's legacy became somewhat misunderstood; and by the 9th century, her nine works had all but disappeared. She was too lustful even for the Romans, and rumours abound that her writing was destroyed by a censorious pope or an illiberal establishment who had come to see her inspired works as morally dangerous. Worst of all, they were created by a woman. All that was left was a series of fragments, literary echoes on scraps of papyrus, the odd line or quote pieced together from others' works. Still, the 'Sapphic stanza' influenced later poets throughout the Middle Ages and beyond.

For many years, it was thought that only one piece had been preserved in its entirety – the deliciously queer 'Ode to Aphrodite' – and other texts known as 'fragments'. Then, in 1879, a discovery was made: scraps of papyrus dug up from an Ancient Egyptian rubbish tip turned out to be poetry from Sappho, Sophocles and Euripides. Suddenly, more fragments and lines could be attributed to her, and her power as a canonical writer grew. In 2017, a private collector in London produced a scrap of papyrus, discovered in a mummy wrapping, that was recognized as definitively Sappho. A poem about her brothers and a fragment of a piece about unrequited love were discovered, expanding what we know about this ancient poet. But it is precisely the fact that Sappho's work exists only in fragments that has tantalized her followers and fans, who search for meaning in the spaces between her own words.

There are many versions of Sappho. Over the centuries, academics have borrowed from the vogueish issues of the time to decipher who she truly was. Some think of her as a cult or coven leader, others see her as a passionate educator of women, and many see Sappho as the head of a social group of extraordinary females, deftly documenting their love-ins and fallings-out. Although some academics doubt that Sappho was truly a lesbian herself (after all, the concepts of sexuality and homosexuality are relatively modern), it is generally accepted that her work celebrates love and desire between women. In recent times, resistance to the idea that Sappho was a lesbian has been met with healthy, queer-minded scepticism. Her works are passionate and full-blooded and read like lesbian flirt texts: 'You came, and I was longing for you; you cooled my heart which was burning with desire,' says Sappho. 'As soon as I glance at you a moment, I / can't say a thing, / and my tongue stiffens into silence, thin / flames underneath my skin prickle and spark, / a rush of blood booms in my ears, and then / my eyes go dark.'

Today, with Sappho's words calling to women everywhere, both her feminist and erotic qualities are thought of as the core of her work. Naturally, her homeland – Lesbos itself – has become something of a magnet for lesbians and their friends. Skala Eresou, close to Sappho's birthplace, is a tiny fishing village on the west coast of the Greek isle. It has welcomed Sapphic devotees openheartedly for decades, complete with annual women's festival, lesbian-owned bar, tarot workshops and a naked beach. Lesbian heaven is a place on earth.

APOLLO

The kaiju[1]-slaying sex-positive superbeing

A sex-positive superbeing of the Ancient Greek pantheon, Apollo is the ancient god of sunbathing, club remixes, wrestling, sailors and man-to-man love and desire. One of the Twelve Olympians, son of Zeus and twin brother of Artemis (his super-queer sister), Apollo is the handsome, longhaired god of the sun and music, champion Olympic wrestler and lauded lyre-player. His list of patronage is impressive, and he is the protector of young men. He is one of the main players of the Olympians, and in the ancient mythical stories it is Apollo who has all the fun. He slays giants and a monstrous kaiju-like python, has countless sexual partners, and his origin story is that of the ultimate golden boy. Apollo was born with a sword in his hand; swans circled his island home seven times in celebration of his birth

---

1   Kaiju are the giant monsters of the Japanese film and TV genre of the same name.

and a waft of ambrosial fragrance ebbed over the land. He grew to become the ultimate example of physical perfection, the ideal of kouros – the tall, lithe and beardless youth the Greeks so venerated – with a laurel crown resting on his handsome head.

There are nine sublime and very queer mythical stories from which to draw conclusions about Apollo's sexuality. That's nine male lovers, each with his own passionate Apollo story, although almost all end tragically (as most ancient gay stories do). The most famous is Apollo's tryst with Hyacinthus, the achingly beautiful Spartan prince for whom Apollo and wind god Zephyrus shared an obsession. As Andrew Calimach writes in *Lovers' Legends*, ' "That boy will be mine," let fly Apollo, an edge to his voice.' Of course it was Apollo who won Hyacinthus; but later, as the lovers tried their hand at discus, Zephyrus was able to enact his revenge. 'The two stripped naked,' imagines Calimach, 'sleeked their skin with smooth olive oil, the better to glisten in the light, and stepped out in the field.' When Hyacinthus throws his discus high into the sky it is Zephyrus who blows it down again, bludgeoning the young prince in the head, which hangs from his neck, lolling down towards the earth, the ground stained with blood. After mourning his death, Apollo creates a flower on the same spot.

Not every male lover of Apollo ended his days with a floral tribute. Branchus, a lusty young shepherd known for being the most handsome man in Greece, happened upon Apollo in the woods and, somewhat starstruck, kissed the sun god. Apollo rewarded his devotion by gifting him the power of prophecy, along with a crown and a magical staff.

Apollo's power echoes through the centuries, his perfect form reflected in ancient sculpture and classical art. Some have used the handsome god's popularity to explore queer perspectives, even if those meanings can lie hidden, coded within the work itself. In this way, love and desire between men can be depicted through versions of Apollo, even in times and places where the subject might be forbidden. Italian artist Marcantonio Raimondi explored just this in his brave engraving *Apollo and His Lover* (1506), featuring the god and his male companion locked in a sensual embrace, and in the Vatican stands the *Apollo Belvedere*, a marble sculpture created in 120–140 CE. The piece represents Apollo, having just fired off an arrow that has slayed the kaiju python, standing tall and proudly and unapologetically nude.

The *Apollo Belvedere* is thought to be the inspiration behind the focus by artists on anatomy and physicality during the Renaissance; the statue was beloved by Michelangelo and piqued the interested of 18th-century scholar Johann Winckelmann, who wrote about the statue's intense, erotic power. From a contemporary viewpoint, Winckelmann had a rather queer outlook (his private love letters show his love and desire for several nubile young men) and his exuberant, gay fanfic-like descriptions of art make for steamy reading. To Winckelmann, the mouth of the *Apollo Belvedere* was 'shaped like that whose touch stirred with delight the loved Branchus', invoking one of Apollo's male lovers, and 'the soft hair plays about the divine head as if agitated by a gentle breeze, like the slender waving tendrils of the noble vine'. Winckelmann's writings were hugely influential, and by the mid-1800s *Apollo B*'s was considered the hottest torso in town.

Later, the god appears in Jean Cocteau's lively, homoerotic creations, and even inspires gay male societies like the Mystic Krewe of Apollo in New Orleans, established in 1969. Robert Mapplethorpe's black-and-white portrait of a sculpture of Apollo attempts to distil the god's beauty, sexuality and perfection into one image. Mapplethorpe, the American photographer known for his male and female nudes, focus on S&M subcultures and penis portraits, drew on classical sculpture in his work. 'If I had been born one or two hundred years ago,' he said, 'I might have been a sculptor, but photography is a very quick way to see, to make sculpture.' His *Apollo* (1988) at the Guggenheim Museum in New York is a close-cropped image of a pale marble statue of Apollo himself, focusing on the god's impossibly perfect face.

BAUBO

Legendary goddess of mirth, magic and muff-flashing

There are as many versions of the Baubo myth as there are shapes of vulvas, but the GOAT (greatest of all time) places Baubo, ancient goddess of mirth and muff-flashing, as a middle-aged nurse at the court of King Celeus of Eleusis. Demeter, the goddess of the harvest and major player of the Olympians, was a palace guest who desperately grieved for her daughter, Persephone. Stolen by Hades, Persephone had been condemned to live forever in the underworld and Demeter's intense sadness had cast a shadow across the world. Seeing her in the depths of depression, Baubo did what she could to bring light and laughter to the situation. So, how did she attempt to improve the goddess's mood? By yanking up her skirt and flashing her nether regions at her.

In the early Orphic religion, Baubo was a side character, a bit part in the mythos of the ancient world, and a comic aside who the writers of the Eleusinian mysteries might have assumed would disappear into obscurity. But she grew powerful, becoming synonymous with other female and fertility deities, and was beloved in many households. She was thought to ward off evil and even had her own merch: Baubos were mass-produced small comic figurines with the character's exaggerated vulva on display. And why not? Statues of Pan or Dionysus are often eye-wateringly phallic; Baubo's magical parts surely deserved the same veneration.

Much of what we know of Baubo's origins comes from Greek Christian writer Clement of Alexandria (150–215 CE) and his whiny *Exhortation to the Greeks*. A professional complainer, Clement was responsible for rambling moralistic critiques, particularly focused on the Orphic religion. In his shrill tone he recorded many stories of the era, accidentally revealing more of Baubo's backstory just as she revealed her 'secret parts' with 'shamelessness'. An early example of slut-shaming that echoed through the centuries.

How to interpret Baubo's vulva-flashing gesture? And the creation of Baubo herself? To the moralistic cultures that followed, and to men like Clement, Baubo's skirt-lifting seemed bawdy and unwomanly. Was it merely a joke or a show of solidarity? Or perhaps a reminder of female sexual power, of renewal and creation? Clement couldn't quite grasp the Greek's notion of *anasyrma*, the ritual lifting of a skirt or tunic, and the flash of nakedness that might ward off evil spirits. Baubo's act of flashing to distract or mock, or as a heartstopping reset, has been the practice of female protestors and activists for centuries. In modern times, Jayna Zweiman and Krista Suh's bright-pink pussy hats were worn proudly at the landmark women's march in Washington, DC in 2017. Groups like FEMEN, the Euro feminist collective that originated in Ukraine, protest topless at patriarchal and exclusionary events (like storming the stage, bare-chested, during a talk on women at a religious conference that included no women). 'Manifestation of the right to her body by the woman is the first and the most important step to her liberation,' say FEMEN over at femen.org. 'Female nudity [is a] sacral symbol of women's liberation.' And Iranian author and activist Maryam Namazie has also practised *anasyrma* to protest in defence of women's rights in the Middle East and North Africa. Both FEMEN and Namazie have received abuse for their dissent.

But in all the old stories, Baubo is the joker, the sacred fool or trickster archetype present in so many mythological systems. She was even a character in Ancient Grecian festivals, with a male priest-like figure dressing as Baubo and lifting his skirt in comic relief. These characters are always underestimated, but they have surprising power and influence

– and in the case of Baubo, she has come to represent an unabashed sexuality (the Ancient Greek word for dildo, *baubon*, derives from Baubo herself), humour and female power. No wonder she is considered the goddess of mirth and magic and – through her feminist ways – has a special place in the lesbian mythical universe.

What happened after Baubo so expertly flashed her esteemed and grieving guest? It seems that the best jokes are the risky ones: Demeter laughed so hard and was so much lighter of spirit that she became bold enough to call upon Zeus to help broker her beloved daughter's release. The Baubo of myth embodies comedy, solidarity, transformation and unapologetic sexual energy, and flashes it all in an act of astonishing, infinite vulva-power.

GANYMEDE

Michelangelo's legendary obsession and the immortal male lover of Zeus

In 1532, Michelangelo met Tommaso dei Cavalieri, the brattish young son of an Italian nobleman. Days later, he sent Tommaso *The Rape of Ganymede*, his lively sketch of the infamous ancient myth in black chalk on brownish paper. The work shows a nude, musclebound man being stolen from the ground by a massive anthropomorphic eagle and soaring off into the clouds. In the myth, the oversized eagle is old Zeus himself, besotted with the young Ganymede, but in Michelangelo's depiction there is no fear in the kidnapped man's eyes. In fact, he is in ecstasy.

The sketch, with all its lusty 1980s fantasy-art vibes, is full of drama, and Michelangelo, then a celebrity artist pushing 60, thought it might encourage Tommaso to learn to draw himself. Over the years, the pair exchanged letters and Michelangelo sent Tommaso passionate sonnets and other muscly hero sketches, and they became friends for life. But that first sketch, with Ganymede's thick thighs pulled apart by the eagle's claws, his face in rapture, is generally considered homoerotic in the extreme. To most art historians, it is clear that Michelangelo was effectively sliding into Tommaso's DMs.

Let's swap Tommaso for Prince Ganymede, the most handsome man in all of Troy. A skilled hunter and natural athlete, Gany had his own fan club, including Zeus, king of the gods. And 'The more Zeus looked at Ganymede, the brighter the fire of his love burned,' writes Andrew Calimach in *Lovers' Legends*. Soon, Zeus's passion was at fever pitch. The great god transformed into an eagle, conjured a thunderstorm for dramatics, and plucked the young man from the ground to take him high into the sky, Ganymede's pet dog barking mournfully after him. The pair flew to Mount Olympus, where, writes Calimach, Zeus 'kept the blond prince for his beloved and took him to his bed'.

The myth has inspired artists for centuries, some imagining Ganymede as a strapping young man and others – creepily – perceiving him as much younger. In fact, there are many different versions of Gany's story. Sometimes he is a herdsman, other times a debutante, but all end with him being taken and transformed into a godlike figure. He becomes Zeus's cup bearer and lover and is given the gift of immortality, with Zeus compensating his family for his kidnapping with a set of magical horses.

If Ganymede's defining moment in ancient myth is Zeus's dominion over him, there are other, lesser stories that show a different side to the immortal prince. As a member of the immortals, he was able to befriend Eros, the god of love and sex, and there are tales of Ganymede's fury when the mischievous god cheated him in a game of chance. He is also the only one of Zeus's lovers made immortal.

Almost all of those artists who have engaged with the story have looked to the immortal prince as a symbol of male-to-male love and desire, the notion of consent conveniently ignored in favour of the thrill of the chase. He first appeared on pottery some time in the 5th century, skipping gracefully across bowls and kraters (large, urn-like vases), often holding a cockerel – a gift of heavy-handed symbolism thought to be given by an older suitor to his male object of desire. But it was Michelangelo's era, the Renaissance, where Ganymede-mania took over. He popped up in Spanish theatre and in Marlowe's *Dido, Queen of Carthage* (1587–1593), and Shakespeare had great fun subverting the legend in *As You Like It* (1599), using Ganymede to blur gender boundaries and confuse and delight the audience. In this comic play, the character Rosalind dresses as the male Ganymede to get close to the object of her affection, Orlando, but accidentally piques the interest of shepherdess Phoebe. As boys played the part of female characters in the 1500s, contemporary stagings of *As You Like It* had boys doing girls doing boys, all orbiting around the idea of Ganymede, a mythical story that Renaissance audiences were well versed in.

Other painters such as Michelangelo's contemporary Antonio da Correggio and, some time later, Johann Wilhelm Baur, were also inspired by the legend. Much has been written about these artists' depictions and about the meaning of Ganymede's grasp of the eagle's wing; and Baur's version shows the prince grabbing the bird and riding it into the sky. To later artists, Ganymede's flying off into the clouds seemed to suggest some sort of ascension, a spiritual awakening – Gany getting high. But to Michelangelo, Ganymede embodied something quite simple: the anxieties and pleasures of desire, not *falling* in love, but soaring with it up to the heavens.

ZEUS

The supremely problematic power-daddy of the Greek gods

The busiest bisexual the mythical world has ever known, Zeus is king of the sky and thunder, lord of Olympus, ruler of the gods and serial heartbreaker of the ancient world – he's the ultimate power-daddy. The capricious god is at the centre of countless myths, epic poems and stories, hell-bent on using his near-infinite power to take whatever and whomever he wants, regardless of consent or consequence. He's . . . a lot.

Linked to the sun, the sky and lightning, Zeus's name seems to be derived from the Ancient Greek word for 'bright', and his iconography includes the eagle, the bull and the oak tree. Classical statues have him oversized and imposing, holding a sceptre in one hand and grasping a thunderbolt in his other fist. He is strong and mature, thought of as the big daddy of the pantheon, and the ultimate authority passing down harsh judgement (in art, depictions of Zeus and the Christian god are

startlingly similar). But he is also a toxic mess, impulsive and fickle; and as the ultimate philanderer he has scores of offspring.

Perhaps Zeus is less queer than voracious, less hero than villain; endless stories of his seduction techniques, although deliciously weird, are also tales of violation, male dominion, sexual trickery and abuse. A theme uniting his endless conquests is transformation: the god king would happily morph into vapour, a flame, a shower of gold or any number of animals in order to nestle into the breasts of those who would otherwise reject his advances. When he had his eye on Leda, the wife of King Tyndareus, he turned into a swan seeking refuge from an eagle and 'seduced' her (after which she laid two eggs); and on seeing beautiful Europa, he became a friendly, bashful bull so as to nose under her toga. As just discussed, to steal handsome Prince Ganymede he turned into an eagle before whisking him off up into the sky (see page 55). His insatiable lust made him rather busy, and his conquests were both women and men. Of all his many lovers and victims, it was only Ganymede to whom he gave the gift of immortality.

There can be no Zeus without his antagonist. Although many of the stories cast Prometheus (the Titan who stole fire and more to give to the humans) as Zeus's arch-enemy, it is Zeus's wife, Hera, who thwarts his every move. Linked to fertility and childbirth, and the guardian of marriage, Hera is a more ancient god than Zeus (she is thought to be the first deity to have inspired a closed-roof temple, in 800 BCE). Although she appears in almost all the Zeus stories, depictions of Hera verge on the misogynistic. At best, she is nagging and nit-picking and at worst insanely and psychopathically jealous and vengeful. She is the fear in Zeus's eyes, the force behind his reluctant and infrequent moral choices and the adversary to his every mythical moment. After a drugging attempt goes awry, Hera is no longer able to fight Zeus and instead turns her hatred on his extramarital conquests. Zeus is such a strong force that the ancient storytellers barely awarded his long-suffering wife a name: 'Hera' translates as merely 'mistress' or 'lady'.

She is one of seven wives that Zeus has in his lifetime, many of whom are, like Hera, Zeus's close relatives or siblings (a fact oddly glossed over in the epic poems). In art, Hera is presented as beautiful, matronly and a lover of animals. In fact, Zeus transformed himself into a cuckoo to flutter about her breasts – and when he revealed his true form she was so embarrassed she agreed to marry him. According to Callimachus, the 300 BCE poet and scholar, their wedding feast lasted 3,000 years. (Don't wedding receptions always feel that way?)

Zeus inspired several patriarchal cults in ancient times, with altars and offerings elbowing their way into spaces reserved for other, even older deities. He was thought to have been born in

Crete, and statues discovered on the island show a handsome, longhaired youth. But Zeus had a darker side too. Every nine years on Mount Lykaion in Arcadia a rather creepy offering was made to him, with evidence of human sacrifice; and then came Zeus-themed oracle sites, before he became the tempestuous, bearded patriarch we know and love to hate.

With sculpture and neoclassical art giving Zeus regal supreme-being realness, moviemakers have been keen to follow suit. Niall MacGinnis played him as a portly king in *Jason and the Argonauts* (1963); Laurence Olivier stooped so low as to appear as the great sky god in marvellous monster mash-up *Clash of the Titans* (1981), a role reprised by a soft-focus Liam Neeson in the 2010 reboot; chiselled Luke Evans took over in the hyper-camp *Immortals* (2011); and Russell Crowe played Zeus for belly laughs in *Thor: Love and Thunder* (2022). That same year, the big guy himself, Arnold Schwarzenegger, also announced that he was taking the form of the sky god in a mysterious upcoming project, furiously exciting myth bros for what might be the best depiction of Zeus yet. It turned out to be a car commercial.

HERMAPHRODITUS

The enchanted two-sexed hero of the Greek pantheon

In the Musée du Louvre lies a life-sized marble sculpture of a naked figure in erotic repose. The subject, created in the 2nd century CE, sleeps on an impossibly plump mattress (added in 1620 by Gian Lorenzo Bernini and biscuit-tufted like a Chesterfield). The viewer, it seems, is meant to approach from the rear, to first see the figure's big, heavy butt cheeks glowing like the full moon. The repose, the robe slipped off and delicately draped over the figure's calves, the long, pinned-up hair, fine limbs and face and the bum itself all read as indisputably female. But view the piece from the other side to see that the figure leans over slightly to reveal not just the swell of a breast but also the somewhat surprising addition of a penis.

The sculpture is the *Sleeping Hermaphroditus*, one of nine in museums and private collections around the world and thought to have been one of hundreds in ancient times. It would have been a conversational piece, something to ponder over at elite events, and it is inspired by the myth of Hermaphroditus, which was one of the first stories to challenge dominant notions of gender and the way we view and categorize the human body. Although the *Sleeping* sculpture might seek to surprise and delight, it also forces the viewer to rethink what might have always been assumed.

The son of Aphrodite and Hermes, Hermaphroditus was an incredibly handsome young man, or so the legend goes; he had Hermes' athletic strength and huge set of guns, and Aphrodite's beauty and affinity with others. When he was old enough, he set about to travel the world. When the naiad (a type of nymph) Salmacis spotted him near her enchanted pool, she instantly fell in love, although shy Hermaphroditus did not feel the same. But, as is the case in so many of the Ancient Greek myths, Salmacis was not deterred. Some versions of the story describe a scuffle in the woods, even a passion-fuelled near-drowning, between the naiad and her obsession.

After spurning Salmacis's attention, and thinking himself alone, Hermaphroditus decides to go skinny-dipping in her pool. But Salmacis, having secretly watched the young man undress, grabs at him in the water. Thrashing about, the naiad calls out to the gods. She can't bear to ever be parted from Hermaphroditus and the gods answer her call, but perhaps not in the way that she means. Plot twist: they fuse the two together. When Hermaphroditus emerges from the enchanted water he is transformed – no longer just a mere man, but both a man and a woman.

Hermaphroditus's two sexes and the Greek hero's dramatic transformation have had artists and writers hot and bothered for centuries. Relics from the ancient world show pottery, frescoes and sculptures depicting many versions of the character, with painters enjoying the mash-up of characters, bodies and sexes. While in Book 4 of Ovid's *Metamorphoses* the myth reads as a harsh warning – a bashful male punished by losing his masculine prowess and a lusty female erased by her own passion – artists apparently didn't get the memo. Sculptures show a bosomed man here, a bearded Aphrodite there, and a nearly nude Hermaphroditus letting it all hang out at nap time. And today, fantasy fan artists return to the myth again and again. This is because parts of the Hermaphroditus myth feel utterly contemporary: this blurring of gender, and a reconsidering of how we look at the human body, is part of our ongoing cultural conversation. As gender becomes increasingly re-examined, medical magic has allowed some of us to venture into Salmacis's enchanted waters and physically transform into the person we may know ourselves to be.

In all this flurry of Hermaphroditus art, Salmacis herself is often overlooked. Casting a female character with true sexual desire was at odds with many of the ancient stories and she is often portrayed as monstrous in her pursuit of Hermaphroditus. And yet, a description on some wall remains in Halicarnassus, Greece, describes Salmacis as the young man's much-loved nurse and carer. Perhaps the ancient writers got it wrong? There are so few artworks and imaginings of the naiad's backstory – and what becomes of her when she is fused and then absorbed into Hermaphroditus's form?

In the end, it might not have been Ovid or the creator of the Louvre's *Sleeping Hermaphroditus* who said it best. The Spice Girls' '2 Become 1' (1996) is perhaps the most prescient artistic work on which to imagine the true voice of Salmacis. You can almost hear her singing to the naked form of Hermaphroditus himself, mournful notes at dusk that drift across her enchanted pool: 'Any deal that we endeavour / Boys and girls feel good together / Take it or leave it, take it or leave it / Are you as good as I remember, baby? / Get it on, get it on / 'Cause tonight is the night when two become one.'

TEIRESIAS

Multiversal gender-magician and sex therapist to the gods

Teiresias lived and loved in a multitude of worlds, genders, abilities and thrillingly weird narratives. They blurred boundaries, broke hearts, hated copulating snakes and used birds and ghosts to tell the future: they were the multiversal magus of ancient times. Of all the many appearances of Teiresias in mythological stories, three overlapping versions show us how delightfully complex this character was. If the overused academic buzzword 'liminal' is good for anything, it is to describe Teiresias.

They (they/them pronouns work perfectly for Teiresias) once were the son of Everes, a friendly shepherd (in Ancient Greek his name means 'well-fitted') and the nymph Chariclo, the beautiful BFF of Athena. The first version of their story takes place on a hike in the mountains where Teiresias spied a pair of writhing snakes having sex (because, why not?) and saw fit to whack them with a stick. Hera, clearly a snake-lover, was furious and as a punishment used her magical powers to transform the son of Everes and Chariclo into a woman. Not one to waste an opportunity, Teiresias soon moved up the ranks and became a priestess of Hera and lived for seven years in their newly acquired gender, falling in love with men and bearing children, including their daughter Manto, a well-known fortune-teller. Centuries later, the Hellenic writers further explored Teiresias's seven female years, expanding their story into a seven-episode boxset with rom-com themes and a string of mishaps and male lovers. But for the season finale featuring a clever call-back, Teiresias saw another set of cavorting snakes on their path. This time, they resisted the temptation to strike them – and was then transformed into a man.

This genderplay overlaps the character's second narrative: that of Teiresias as the ancient world's most successful prophet, although one who can see only with their mind, not their eyes. Echoing the story of Actaeon and Artemis, Teiresias stumbles upon Athena as she bathes naked in a pond, and for their accidental insolence they are transformed, losing the power of sight. On hearing their mother Chariclo's sadness, her friend Athena gives Teiresias a gift: the power to see into the future. Some stories have Teiresias as a dedicated bird-fancier, interpreting their chirping as messages from the future, a gift known as 'augury'; but in all cases, Teiresias becomes the best fortune-teller this side of Mount Olympus.

A third version of Teiresias and the transformation of their sight is a comic tale of Hera and Zeus. Bickering about who enjoys sex more, men or women, they turn to Teiresias to settle the argument. Hera claims that a man must enjoy sex more than a woman, and Zeus is convinced of the opposite. Teiresias, being in a unique position of having experienced both, claims that a man only feels a tenth of what a woman does. Hera, again in fury, removes Teiresias's sight but Zeus gives them their famous prophesizing powers to make up for it.

Either way, Teiresias – in their new masc-presenting form – appears in several ancient stories as prophecy's GOAT. In fact, their name became a stand-in for any fortune-teller in almost every Greek legend. They guest-star in the Narcissus/ Hyacinthus myth as the prophet who claims he will live a long and happy life so long as he doesn't know himself, and pops up in *Odyssey*, Book 11, to commune with the dead (which was Teiresias's preferred way to divine). In the legend of Oedipus, they appear in terrifying fashion, with foolish Oedipus thinking he knows better than Teiresias themselves. A murder, suicide, incest and eye-gouging later, Oedipus learns the hard way that Teiresias's predictions are almost always tragic – and are always right.

In these ancient stories, Teiresias moves back and forth through time and genders, through seeing and unseeing, and through the known and unknown. They live in both the immortal world, as priestess of Hera, and the real world, bearded and holy, sharing their infuriatingly riddle-like prophecies with humankind. This liminality – especially across gender – has inspired artists and writers for centuries. Teiresias is thought to be one of the inspirations behind Virginia Woolf's *Orlando: A Biography* (1928), the story of a character who lives many lives and two sexes and is themselves a modern literary mythological character. The myth was also explored in 2011 in a stunning work of endurance art called *Tiresias* that has been staged many times since. Here, transgender artist Cassils used their naked body, itself muscular and lithe; wearing a neoclassical Greek male torso made of ice, they allow their body heat to melt the sculpture over four hours, transforming in front of their audience's eyes. 'Embodying the holy man's double gender,' Cassils has said, '. . . fully male and fully female, was important for his prophecies and his experiences.'

Counting the many, many mythical appearances of Teiresias, it's clear that the Ancient Greeks revered them; they were the rock star of prophesizing. Perhaps they knew that Teiresias's magical ability to see beyond the veil was because they lived life as both male and female, and that it was a gift.

IPHIS AND IANTHE

The ancient queer lovers and their ingenious blurring of gender boundaries

Another gender-reveal party goes horribly wrong. At the birth of Iphis, there were no embarrassing piñata accidents, dead doves, a misfiring canon, or $8 million of bushfire damage, but instead a murder thwarted with moments to spare. Ovid wrote about Iphis's incredible beginnings in *Metamorphoses*, breathlessly describing how the character only survived due to an act of divine intervention and an ingenious blurring of gender boundaries.

In the story, Ovid takes us to ancient south-central Crete and the family home of Ligdus, a seemingly sweet man of humble ways. When his wife, Telethusa, became pregnant, Ligdus wished dearly for a boy. A girl would have meant scrabbling together a dowry the couple could ill-afford. He came to a horrifying conclusion: that he must kill the baby should it be a girl. So far, so Ancient Greek.

Telethusa cried out to the gods and one night was visited by Isis, goddess of healing and magic, and her team of infanticide avengers. Isis's Egyptian super-crew were Osiris (god of the underworld), Anubis (the jackal-headed god of the dead), Bastet (the cat woman of ancient times) and shy little Apis (the god of silence). They had a message for the pregnant woman: have your baby and we will protect you. Of course, the baby born was a girl but Telethusa, emboldened by her godly visit, concealed the baby's sex and told Ligdus that he now had the son he'd always wished for. He named the baby Iphis, after his grandfather.

Iphis grew into a handsome and popular youth and soon met Ianthe, the hottest girl in school. The pair fell madly in love and here's where it gets tricky – or *trickier*. Iphis and Ianthe wanted to marry but Iphis, knowing their sex was female, saw that marriage was out of the question. Iphis felt as though they were doomed. In some versions of the story, it is Telethusa who again calls to the gods for their help and in others it is Iphis – but either way their prayer is (again) answered. On the night before the wedding, Iphis is magically transformed into a male and the ceremony goes ahead as planned, with gods in attendance.

The Iphis and Ianthe legend is fascinating in its ancient portrayal of queer love, gender and sexuality. Before their transformation, female Iphis's love for Ianthe is full-blooded and real and – for many myth readers – lesbian. But the character, both before and after their wedding day, might also be read as trans. It's . . . complicated.

This complexity has drawn the attention of artists and writers across the centuries. Ovid, who would occasionally stray into moral judgement of his subjects, elsewhere writes disparagingly about lesbian love. Here, for example, Ovid imagines Iphis in true gay panic. In a translation by Tony Kline, he writes: 'Hardly restraining her tears, she said "What way out is there left, for me, possessed by the pain of a strange and monstrous love, that no one ever knew before?" ' In this telling, even though Iphis is rewarded with what they truly desire – marriage to Ianthe – they must become male to achieve it.

Ovid had a habit of transforming characters when he thought their behaviours too problematic and he certainly wrote from a patriarchal and penis-focused perspective. The notion of female–female desire was somewhat mystifying to the male writers of his time, but Ovid goes on to write passionately about Iphis's love for Ianthe: 'love had touched both their innocent hearts . . . Iphis loved one whom she despaired of being able to have, and this itself increased her passion, a girl on fire for a girl.'

In 2007, British author Ali Smith remixed Ovid's tale in her short novel *Girl Meets Boy*. In the story, two sisters, Imogen and Anthea, grow up hearing the Ovidian tale of Iphis from their grandfather. Later, as adults living in their dear departed grandparents' house, freewheeling Anthea falls in love with Robin, a genderqueer activist. When Anthea meets Robin, she sees that 'She was as meaty as a girl. She was as graceful as a boy. She was as brave and handsome and rough as a girl. She was as pretty and delicate and dainty as a boy.' Anthea and Robin's desire for each other, and Robin's queerness, challenges Imogen, but eventually it awakens and inspires the uptight sister, transforming her life into one of joy.

In both versions of the mythical story, love wins. But in the original, Iphis's true nature is hidden from all but themselves, their mother and the gods. The characters in *Girl Meets Boy* live their lives out in the open instead. Smith brings the idea of queer visibility to the Iphis myth, exploring how queer love can be life-changing, that it might magically inspire and ultimately transform anyone who witnesses it.

GILGAMESH AND ENKIDU

Godly guys grappling: the world's most ancient erotic gay love story

Back 4,000 years to the 3rd century BCE and perhaps the first queer tale ever told: *The Epic of Gilgamesh* – which is also thought to be the world's most ancient written story. The oldest version was found in 1867 in the complex cuneiform text pieced together from tens of thousands of clay fragments that had been gathering dust in the storeroom of the British Museum. When he first translated it, George Smith, a self-taught layman the museum had taken under its wing ten years before, stripped off naked in excitement, and the world too was enthralled. Smith thought he had found a passage of text in the reconstructed clay tablets that might prove the story of Genesis – a hot topic at a time when the Bible's historicity was in doubt – but he was wrong. It was the erotic tale of King Gilgamesh and his burly and so-very-hairy best buddy, Enkidu. When it's clay, it's gay.

The story is a classic hero's quest with buddy-movie elements and is heavy on bromance, but it is the seemingly erotic language used to describe its two male protagonists that has encouraged some to see this epic story through a rainbow-coloured lens. With a moon goddess for a mother, King Gilgamesh has always hoped for his own godly powers but is just a mere mortal. His sense of inadequacy makes him a sloppy, distracted and disastrous monarch that his long-suffering subjects hope soon to be rid of. But one night he dreams of a beautiful star falling to earth, one he struggles to carry, and his mother tells him it is a sign that his soulmate will soon appear. He then meets Enkidu, a wild bear of a man, and their tragic relationship teaches Gilgamesh to finally accept his true nature.

So far, so queer, and there are other aspects of the story of these two male friends that feel more like gay desire than brotherly horseplay. When Gilgamesh and Enkidu first meet, they famously wrestle, throwing each other about like a damp loincloth. Only when Gilgamesh sees that he has finally met his equal do they call off the oily grappling; then they kiss and become BFFs. They go on to defeat a demon, anger a goddess and survive an attack from a magical bull, which they slay in the process, and the gods eventually kill Enkidu as punishment. Gilgamesh is left distraught and 'acting like a widow'.

As with almost all 'Are they or aren't they?' relationships of myth, some scholars have struggled to accept that queerness might be hidden in the ancient clay text; Gilgamesh studies have been fraught with fallings-out over this very issue. But some point to the fact of the author's constant referrals to the king's need to 'love and embrace' his friend Enkidu 'like a wife'. And then there's the intense sexual prowess of both men. Although they don't actually get it on, their union has erotic overtones – it's full of wrestling and rolling around in its early days and then develops into a more spiritual connection. Another scholar points to the men's soulmate status: theirs is an endless love that ultimately transforms their life. Gay Catholic writer Terence Weldon says in his essay 'Queer Gods, Demigods and Their Priests: The Middle East' that the Gilgamesh–Enkidu way – wrestle and kiss now, fall in love later – 'will be familiar to many modern gay men. In place of the romantic stereotype of a slowly blossoming chaste courtship, followed by a grand wedding and only then by sexual consummation, the pattern is more usually reversed.'

In the end, Gilgamesh travels to the underworld to claim back his lost love, but he fails and is finally forced to accept his mortal limits. He has changed; and just at this point, he hears Endiku's voice echoing from the afterlife. The most ancient tale in the world is a tale of queer-edged love, everlasting.

NIANKHKHNUM AND KHNUMHOTEP

The celebrated queer husbands of an Ancient Egyptian metropolis

To Egypt now and the ancient village of Saqqara, less than an hour south of Cairo. Close to the green banks of the Nile, Saqqara is given over to desert sands, crumbling pyramids, eight million animal mummies and the world's oldest complete complex of stone buildings. It once served as the necropolis for the old Egyptian capital, Memphis, but in recent decades Saqqara has welcomed a new, slightly more alive community. It is now home to full-time archaeologists, scholars, hieroglyph experts and queer tour groups hoping to catch a glimpse of a monument to what is thought to be the first recorded gay male couple in antiquity.

Like all the best queer history, at Saqqara the action is underground. Underneath the pyramids, a series of megatombs – some constructed more than 3,000 years ago – have been slowly uncovered, reconstructed and examined. In the early 1960s, Egyptian archaeologist Ahmed Moussa discovered several of the tombs connected by a rock passageway. And it was Mounir Basta we can thank for crawling through the dusty complex in 1964 to discover something extraordinary: the only tomb in all of Saqqara – and all of Egypt – dedicated to two men. Hieroglyphs and paintings told the story of Niankhkhnum and Khnumhotep, two men with the unenviable (but important) job of tending to the king's nails. The master manicurists are depicted in a series of paintings, at least two of which show them locked in an embrace.

The meaning of the discovery has been fought over ever since: some scholars are convinced the men were brothers, twins in fact, dismissing their nose-to-nose and hand-holding portraits as brotherly love. Others point to the depictions of the men's wives and children – although these are always in the background, which is uncommon in similar tombs. But there are some who think that this embracing pair of handsome and revered male nail-artists, entombed in almost the exact same way as heterosexual couples, were, in fact, lovers.

Imagine the unease in the 1960s about the discovery of potentially queer love hiding in the ruins of Saqqara, and seeing a mural of Khnumhotep delicately sniffing a lotus (traditionally a female act in Ancient Egyptian art). Although the site is often referred to as the Tomb of the Two Brothers, in wall paintings the men share places usually reserved for husband and wife in a banquet scene and the men's names are lovingly interconnected in hieroglyphs.

Gay academic Greg Reeder has long explored the idea that Niankhkhnum and Khnumhotep were lovers, and for decades has hoped to create a more queer-friendly debate in the field. 'It is important for gay people to know that love between two men was beautifully portrayed in an ancient tomb of the 5th Dynasty in Old Kingdom Egypt,' he said in an interview with Dan Vera for *White Crane* journal in 2007. 'The images of them embracing and kissing are stunning reminders that the ancient world has much to teach us about where we have come from; the ways people adapted to the rules of society and yet were still able to express their same-sex devotions.' If Reeder is right, then the relationship between Niankhkhnum and Khnumhotep is truly heroic.

Of course, there are those that contest the idea that the Ancient Egyptians might have venerated a same-sex union, let alone that Niankhkhnum and Khnumhotep were lovers. This includes not only the big-name male historians and Egyptologists of the 1960s, but also the dominant Egyptian culture more generally (Egypt is a very difficult place to be gay).

David O'Connor, an Egyptologist at New York University, has written that the pair might in fact be conjoined twins. And gay historians who specialize in the subject say it simply isn't a done deal and more evidence is needed; hoping something is true does not necessarily mean that it is.

Perhaps the no-nonsense history geeks at the Making Queer History website put it best. 'If a man and woman shared the tomb, the conclusion of a romantic relationship would have been reached immediately,' they say. 'No one would have suggested fraternal conjoined twins, loving siblings, or friendly colleagues. The truth does not require a leap of logic but a small, sensible step forward.' To put it another way, if others cannot accept that gay male love has existed for aeons, and that Ancient Egypt might have had its own sparkling queer mythology, perhaps they are in denial.

ZELDA

The legendary digital deity of gaymers everywhere

For decades, *The Legend of Zelda* has been one of the world's most popular and enduring fantasy role-player video games. After its debut in 1986, the Nintendo adventure has evolved from its charming, lo-fi roots to its current slick, cinematic incarnation. Inspired by European and Japanese myth, J R R Tolkein's Middle Earth, and creator Shigeru Miyamoto's childhood adventures in the hills, forests and hidden caves of Sonobe, Japan, *Zelda* is close to iconic. But fans have often wondered if the game has queer energy hidden in its code – could its titular character even be a lesbian?

The overarching story is thus: Hyrule, one of *Zelda*'s magical lands, is under threat from demon king Ganon. Pointy-eared Link and Princess Zelda herself, a reincarnation of a goddess, must fight to save their home. Ganon wants the Triforce, a powerful and ancient artifact once used by the

goddesses to create Hyrule, to turn the world into darkness, and Link and Zelda will stop at nothing to keep it – and Hyrule – safe. The three characters each represent an aspect of the Triforce and maintaining this uneasy balance is essential, according to the *Zelda* creators.

Players navigate the main *Zelda* world through Link, saving the princess, solving puzzles, fighting demons and helping those in need. Gamers and their queer subcategory, gaymers, love it; and now, decades after the game's first release, *Zelda* houses an incredibly intricate and complex overworld, skipping back and forth through new releases and spinoffs similar to the Marvel Cinematic Universe. Much like the MCU, it is supported by manga adaptations, an official animated series, a wealth of fan art and fanfic, guidebooks, Comic-Con appearances and a whole wishing cap of merch.

As one of the first-ever fantasy role-player video games, *Zelda* has had huge influence on the genre. In a space where players become avatars, changing gender at will to explore mythical worlds full of magic and transformation, is it any wonder they have such a loyal queer following? For this reason, gaymers have long questioned the queerness of *Zelda* and have stepped forth bravely on their own quest to uncover the truth.

Let's first look at the supporting characters. Starring as antagonist in *The Legend of Zelda: Skyward Sword* (2011),

Ghirahim is a sulky, flamboyant demon lord with a swoopy white bob, piercing eyes and a penchant for dramatics. He describes himself as 'stunning' with well-built arms; 'doesn't their shape just leave you . . . breathless?' he croons. The show-off with an extraordinary long and lascivious tongue has many gaymers fizzing with excitement over his evil twink energy. And in *The Legend of Zelda: Breath of the Wild* (2017), we meet Vilia, a queer-femme man and possibly a drag queen, who helps Link sneak into a woman-only town. Also in *Breath of the Wild* we meet Bolson, a queer hippy-daddy with pink headband, eyeliner and a hoop in his right ear (a rather tired old gay myth in itself), and his own incredibly sassy trademark dance. And there was such speculation about Tingle, a male map-seller from *Majora's Mask* (2000) who dresses as a fairy, that Nintendo felt compelled to step in and explain that, no, he's not gay. None of these characters are queer in a particularly straightforward or non-stereotypical way, but they have queer vibes, nonetheless.

There is also a little genderplay in the *Zelda* universe. In *Ocarina of Time* (1989), Zelda hides as a Sheikah boy, named Sheik, causing a mini-meltdown in the gaymer community: had Zelda changed gender? The debate continued for more than two decades until 2014, when Nintendo waded in again to say, no, Sheik is 'simply Zelda in a different outfit'. But that didn't stop fans perceiving the princess as gender nonconforming, possibly trans, or both. To confuse matters further, that same year *Hyrule Warriors* appeared, a *Zelda* spinoff that proudly debuted Linkle, a female version of Link himself – only with a terrible sense of direction. *Zelda*'s hero was suddenly a woman (although a somewhat sexist version at that).

On the eve of *Breath of the Wild*'s release, gaymers finally spoke up and hopeful queer and feminist rumours abounded that the protagonist might be female. Online chatter was fierce, with one tribe pointing their bows and arrows at the dominance of heteronormative gaming and the other sharpening their magical swords to defend it. There were some who claimed that a female main character, and therefore possibility of lesbian love, would disrupt the balance of Triforce (which sounds like a fantasy RPG version of the anti-gay stance lesbians have rolled their eyes at for centuries). In the end, Nintendo execs stepped in once again to set the record (extremely) straight: the central characters of *Zelda* would remain Link, Zelda and Ganon – or in other words, male, female and male. Gaymers were disappointed: in the high-fantasy world of Hyrule, with all its magical gems, swords and incantations, the feeling that anything is possible is hard to shift.

Let's give the gaymers and their allies the last word, break the ancient seal and invoke unauthorized spinoff *The Legend of Gay Zelda* (2017). The fanzine curated by Sara Goetter features works by several *Zelda*-loving queer cartoonists. In the zine, Zelda, Link and a host of minor characters have crushes and fantasies, tentatively hold hands, play with cats and are reimagined as queer. And when Midna from *Twilight Princess* (2006) slips through from the Twilight Realm to spend a day with Zelda, romance blooms and they kiss. It's a work of pure queer magic. In a way, *The Legend of Gay Zelda* answers a question gaymers have pondered for decades: as we tread lightly through the world of *Zelda*, creating our own pathways and journeys, do we not have ownership over our most beloved characters?

TU'ER SHEN

The rebooted queer rabbit god of New Taipei City

To New Taipei City in Taiwan and a busy intersection along Jing'an Road buzzing with mopeds, office workers and shoppers and home to a small, unassuming retail space. Neighbouring a gym, a home-appliance store and posh apartment blocks is something extraordinary: a temple to rabbit god Tu'er Shen and the epicentre of Taiwan's queer religious community.

Inside is a shrine that – pre-pandemic – drew almost 9,000 gay and lesbian Taoist devotees every year. Pilgrims might burn notes of devotion, or offer sploshes of rice wine; their prayers and offerings to the rabbit god are thought to help queer visitors find love, a soulmate and acceptance. But who is this kindly rabbit god? And why is he so beloved by Taiwan's queer community?

We can thank temple founder and priest Lu Wei-ming, who opened the original site in 2006, for helping reignite interest in what was once an overlooked, minor Taoist deity, and making the rabbit god the toast of the town. Although acceptance in Taiwan is growing, and discrimination laws are improving, Lu saw that queer people were still excluded from religious rites and rituals. And so, he drew on a four-century-old legend to bring queer people back to the altar. Lu's idea is that the rabbit god can be seen as the queer counterpart to Yue Xia Lao Ren, the matchmaking deity for straight people.

The legend of the rabbit god is (of course) one of tragedy. According to a Qing dynasty writer, Tu'er Shen wasn't always a deity: he started life as a mortal man known as Hu Tianbao who fell in love with the (extremely handsome) imperial inspector of the Fujian Province. When his unrequited love was discovered, the inspector, aghast, sentenced poor Hu to death. Weeks later, his restless ghost started to appear in others' dreams and the gods took pity on him. He was soon deified and given the job as the guardian of queer love, or so the legend goes. A shrine was erected and became popular in Fujian Province until the cult of Hu Tianbao was suppressed and Tu'er Shen, as he was also known, was all but forgotten.

There is some quibbling among historians over the provenance of the Tu'er Shen myth, and one theory suggests that the whole story is an invention of ancient poet Yuan. Others point to evidence of Hu Tianbao existing at the end of the Ming dynasty and there is clear proof that many worshipped him. So, what of the rabbit connection? In late Imperial Japan, 'rabbit' and 'bunny' were slang terms for gay men. Over the centuries this derogatory term has been reclaimed, overlapping the legend of Tu'er Shen and making him the rabbit god of queer love. Because of his tragic past, and middling fame, it is thought that the rabbit god will try harder for those who truly believe in him. Some visitors are willing to go that extra mile, leaving carrots at the shrine, and others create queer anime-like drawings in his honour, all bulging pecs and bunny ears.

Keeping the rabbit god's legend alive hasn't always been easy. Lu's first shrine, a tiny space down a dark alleyway nearby, was shared with the kitchen doors of local cafés, strings of washing lines, and whirring air-con units; it wasn't quite befitting of the great love god. And soon Lu became unable to accommodate the growing numbers of interested visitors, but he wasn't deterred. He eventually moved the temple to a more upmarket location, bringing the rabbit god and his queer congregation bravely into the light.

It is not all about praying and boyfriend-hunting at the rabbit god's temple. The site has become a focus of Taiwan's queer activist class, emboldened by the country's equal-marriage debate and the ongoing push towards equality. Lu and his congregation have a tough fight on their hands: majority opinion in Taiwan has a conservative bent and local Christians have not been so enamoured with the relaunch of the rabbit god. Protestors have gathered outside the shrine and one religious leader even attempted an exorcism. But the shrine remains, now with online services, digital devotionals and community notices. For many, the rabbit god Tu'er Shen remains the carrot-powered focus of queer love in Taiwan.

LOKI

The chaotic bisexual frat boy
of Norse mythology

Tireless practical joker, party-crasher and chaotic bisexual, Loki is mythology's sloppy frat bro. But the impish, shapeshifting god is also the queer trickster of Nordic legend, a vital figure wrongly marked as evil when he is merely unruly, brilliant and almost always misunderstood (okay, he did kill one of Odin's sons, but that's about it). He skips through the main Nordic legends calling out hypocrisy, ruining parties, and almost singlehandedly brings about Ragnarök . . . aka the end of the world. He is also the protagonist of the pantheon's best morning-after stories, like the time he got pregnant and gave birth to an eight-legged horse – but we'll get to that.

Throughout the ancient epic poems, Loki is the playful Norse god who serves the pantheon but tries to dismantle it at the same time. He marries, has children (including a sea serpent, a wolf and Hel, goddess of the underworld) and

changes sex at will. His female version, an old woman named Pokk, infamously refuses to cry at the death of a god, Loki's frenemy, who would otherwise have been brought back from the dead if the whole world had wept in unison. Loki never does what is hoped for or expected: he's the epitome of shady.

There is something essentially queer about trickster gods like Loki. They have little of the power and privilege of their more dominant counterparts, so they draw on their own resources and use creativity and subterfuge to survive and thrive. In the Nordic pantheon, Loki may not be as stacked or as beloved as Thor, but he can shapeshift and manipulate others to get anything he wants.

One thing about Loki is clear: he's got a mouth on him. In one epic poem, *Lokasenna* from the 10th century, he gets into a 'flyte' – a battle of insults – with the gods. He storms dramatically out of a banquet he wasn't invite to only to return moments later. To the beery crowd he then picks off every guest with comedy roast put-downs, calling one man a 'bench-ornament' and a goddess 'man-crazed', until he wanders drunkenly outside and turns himself into a salmon – because why not?

In another myth, he cuts off Thor's beloved wife Sif's gorgeous golden locks for a laugh and – with apparent regret – promises to employ the dwarf, Ivaldi, to replace it with spun gold. Ivaldi went on to create a host of gifts for the gods, including an ingenious foldable ship and a beautiful spear. Only Loki saw an opportunity to create more mischief: he bet his own handsome head that a pair of rival dwarves, brothers Sindri and Brokk, couldn't better the work of Ivaldi. The pair took up the challenge but kept being bothered and bitten by a fly. Although the brothers managed to create a golden boar and a magical ring that duplicated itself every nine nights, when Brokk created Mjölnir – Thor's magical hammer – the handle was slightly short due to Brokk being bitten on the eye. Loki had won! At the end of his wager, Loki had pocketed six legendary items that each shine out in the Nordic myths, and he only had to shapeshift into a fly to do it.

And then there's the eight-legged horse, Sleipnir. To forfeit a huge payment owed to the builder of a fortress around the gods' home, Loki had to think on his hooves. The builder was only allowed to work single-handedly, with just his lusty stallion, Svadilfari, for help. The gods had thought it an impossible task, but the builder was close to finishing and would soon be owed the sun, the moon and a spare goddess. Loki transformed into a mare and clopped about coquettishly in front of Svadilfari, swishing his tail to distract him. The builder missed the deadline, no bill had to be paid and the gods were finally happy with Loki. But Svadilfari was still keen to have whatever it was the trickster god was offering. Off-page, he did just that, and Loki soon gave birth to Sleipnir, a ghostly grey mega-legged horse. The stallion, a favourite of Odin, could fly – Pegasus-like – through the air.

In recent times, Loki has sparkled darkly in the Marvel Cinematic Universe, his most contemporary incarnation. In it, he is more obviously the god of mischief, with actor Tom Hiddleston evolving the character across films and boxset series from power-crazed prince to a complex, deliciously mischievous and ultimately good-adjacent persona. In the original Marvel comics, Loki flips sex again and embodies Lady Sif, becoming Lady Loki, a character in her own right. In the much-loved Marvel television series *Loki*, he meets a female version of himself, Sylvie (played by Sophia Di Martino), a 'variant' Loki from another timeline. Their love/hate/try-to-murder-each-other relationship is nothing less than charming. In one key scene as they are getting to know each other, Sylvie delicately proposes to Loki that being a prince, there 'must have been would-be princesses . . . or perhaps another prince?' Loki smiles and replies, 'A bit of both.'

CHIN

Penis-powered deity of the Ancient Mayan pantheon

In 1979, Bernabé Pop, a young Q'eqchi' man from Guatemala, at the southern edge of the Maya Mountains in Poptún, stumbled across one of the world's most important archaeological and cultural finds. After his dogs chased an animal into the undergrowth, Bernabé followed, only to find a cave dripping with crystalline stalactites opening onto a large chamber and an astonishing collection of Ancient Mayan rock art, hieroglyphs, inscriptions and artifacts. Some of the artwork dates back 2,000 years, and there was one vignette that has excited queer-minded historians ever since: two men, one with an eye-poppingly large appendage, locked in a passionate embrace. It is thought to be a rare, ancient depiction of the Mayan deity Chin, unofficial guardian of the gays.

Although penises pepper the walls of the caves – now known as Naj Tunich – it is Chin's that is most fascinating. The site, which has been on the UNESCO World Heritage Site shortlist since 2012, has hosted a steady stream of archaeologists, history geeks and looters, since Bernabé's discovery. Many have stopped to wonder WTF Chin is doing.

Most of what we know of Chin – and the ins and outs of the ancient indigenous sexual behaviours of the region – is steeped in colonial thought and creepy theories first put forward by the monks who invaded with the conquistadors in the 16th century. Given the mass book-burning ordered by Bishop Diego de Landa in 1562, the Mayan pantheon is missing an unknowable wealth of stories and wisdom; but what we do know is that the gods of ancient times were deeply involved in all aspects of life. It is thought that there are more than 250 Mayan gods and deities, who together controlled the harvest, health and prosperity, class structure and even the weather; some were also the guardians of social custom, love and sex. Chin is the god – or sometimes goddess – who was councillor to the monarchs, associated with maize, magic and queer making-out. Same-sex love and desire existed – at least in ritual form – in the Ancient Mayan world, and Chin and his or her impressive penis was at the centre of it.

As seen from the artwork at Naj Tunich, Chin didn't like to do it alone. Together with other godly deities, namely Maran, Cu and Cavil, they were usually depicted as demonstrating penis-time with other male gods and humans. But not everyone agrees that the Naj Tunich male-to-male painting is Chin. Andrea J. Stone, who lived in Guatemala in 1980, was able to visit Naj Tunich soon after it was discovered and saw Chin and his appendage with her own eyes. In her book, *Images of the Underworld* (1995), she puts forward another theory: that the painting might depict the Mayan god N, bearer of the universe, and possibly a female counterpart or a man playing the role of a woman in a performance. But the work of feminist archaeologist Rosemary Joyce points out the clear sexualization of the male form in Ancient Mayan art; like the walls at Naj Tunich, it is awash with big penises and scantily clad men, marking out sporty male youths as the must-have ideal of Mayan beauty for both women and men. As Chin is thought to have introduced the idea of male-to-male desire to humans – by showing off his goods – it is more than possible that it is he who features in the paintings at Naj Tunich. Another 16th-century bishop claimed that Chin introduced the idea of gayness by having sex with a demon, but there are no demons at Naj Tunich; this might just be colonial thinking.

Today, Chin and the nobleman (as the other figure in the painting seems to be coded), exist mainly in the minds, memes and fan art of queer-myth devotees. But in Guatemala, Chin's presence is not nearly as powerfully felt as it was in the distant past. It is thought same-sex love enjoyed an uneasy acceptance in ancient times, and that homoeroticism was, apart from being ritualized, associated to some extent with nobility. Colonialism and Christianity changed all that, and gay sex was punishable by death at one point in the country's history. Centuries later, most Guatemalans are members of the Catholic or Protestant churches; those anti-gay attitudes are hard to shift. But queer visibility and acceptance is growing and growing. Perhaps Chin's penis, painted on a cave wall 2,000 years before, still has some of its old magic?

HORUS AND SET

Queer Egyptian mythology's most X-rated frenemies

The tale of Horus and Set, the godly rivals who wrangled and finagled for power over all Egypt following the murder of Osiris, is a vital element in ancient myth. There are many stories of their tempestuous relationship in papyri and paintings, ancient stone reliefs and other artifacts, but one chapter is rather more queer-edged, X-rated – and eye-poppingly weird – than others. This is a story of family fallings-out, Franken-sex, a spiked salad and magical semen.

But first, some background: at one time, Osiris and his wife, Isis (also his sister, but let's ignore that for now), ruled over the land and sky in a golden age of prosperity. Osiris's gnarly little brother, Set, grew jealous of his fame, and chopped him up and scattered the pieces around the world before stealing his role as king. But Isis reassembled Osiris and brought him back to life, Frankenstein-style, for long enough to father a child, Horus.

Within years, Horus was ready to claim his birth right and fight Uncle Set for the throne. What followed was a series of reality-show-style conflicts and competitions – and one rather problematic night together that has piqued the interest of certain Egyptologists ever since the story was discovered.

In 1889, the famous Lahun Papyri collection was discovered in Al Lahun, Egypt, by British Egyptologist Flinders Petrie. Dating from the twelfth dynasty, the papyri are the oldest ever found in the country, and Petrie and his wife Hilda Irwin deciphered their fascinating ancient texts on mathematics, gynaecology and veterinary prowess, and what seems to be one of the oldest chat-up lines in history. In the story, after a series of lost battles against Horus, Set attempts to seduce him, possibly in an attempt to dominate Horus in a new, more creative way. One translation by F Ll Griffith in 1898 reads, 'The Majesty of Set said to the Majesty of Horus: "How beautiful are thy buttocks" ' – which, as a line, is about as direct as it gets. But, as ever, it doesn't go to plan.

After advice from his mother, Isis, young Horus initially declines Set's offer: 'Since you are too heavy for me,' he says, 'my strength will not be equal to yours.' Isis goes on to tell Horus to trick Set into thinking he's had sex with him, going through the motions, as it were, to grab a handful of Set's magical semen. And that's just what he does.

So far, so very weird. Much is written in the ancient texts of Set being duped by Horus's sex-trick and 'losing his seed', as if he had lost all his godly powers in the act. And there are even versions of the story that involve Horus sneaking Set's own magical semen into his favourite salad and serving it up to him. It's more than a little eyebrow-raising.

The idea of historians and Egyptologists of the late Victorian era delicately wading through the story of Set, Horus and the spiked salad is nothing less than hilarious. Some struggled to make the case that conflict between Set and Horus was merely a metaphor; it represented a historical war between two groups of people, not two lusty frenemies creating their own curious porn genre. Some saw the 'losing of' Set's 'seed' as sending the cosmos into chaos, but other scholars seemed to begrudgingly accept that same-sex desire at least existed in ancient times. Of course, there is more queer-edged evidence in the ancient texts, but it tends to be more closely scrutinized than other finds. As we've already learned, when the tomb of male couple Niankhkhnum and Khnumhotep was unearthed at Saqqara, theories that they were brothers or twins dominated for decades (see page 79). The *Book of Dreams* (2nd century BCE) from the Carlsberg Papyrus briefly mentions lesbian sex, but more is made of its prohibition of sex outside marriage.

In recent times, contemporary historians have celebrated queer aspects of the Ancient Egyptian world, and some have reframed how we view the Egypt of old – not always in contrast to Greek or Roman history, but with that of its closer African neighbours. This is queering in its widest and most powerful sense: looking at things from a different perspective in order to uncover new meaning. What's more, this emerging viewpoint might help us understand the sexual attitudes of Ancient Egyptian society, the role same-sex desire played, and early ideas of gender, so that we might understand the Egypt of today, a place of deep inequality with majority conservative attitudes and little legal protection for queer people. But, like the myth of Set and Horus, Egyptian history sparkles with fascinating and mind-bending stories, not all involving salad; the ancient world is just a tiny bit weird and queer whether modern Egypt likes it or not.

BRIGID

The pro-choice feminist triple goddess of myth and legend

Brigid is the flame-haired Irish triple goddess who lived with her female 'soul friend', founded an art school, performed an abortion and could turn water into beer. Originally a member of the Tuatha Dé Danann, the pre-Christian mythical community of gods and goddesses, she has been a pagan priestess, a Catholic saint and a potty-mouthed Haitian Vodou spirit in the centuries her story has been told.

In her first incarnation, Brigid was the goddess of passion and poetry, creativity and childbirth, sun and fire, and was the wife of King Bres, the enemy of the Tuatha Dé Danann. As daughter of the father-god Dagda and Boann, the goddess of fertility, power was Brigid's birth right. Perhaps this is why her name spans the centuries, three mythical universes and some of the most startlingly contemporary stories of women in ancient times. She is a formidable, feminist force to be reckoned with. She even has her own holiday, Imbolc, to mark the midpoint of winter, now celebrated by Celtic pagans and Wiccans and recently recognized as a national holiday in Ireland. And when her son dies in battle, Brigid wails or 'keens' at his graveside, a practice that was followed by women across many cultures until contemporary times.

In the 5th century, Brigid got a Christian rebrand. She transformed from goddess to saint, taking on the form of Brigid of Kildare – a mere human, but one who retained much of her formidable goddess power. Given to a druid as a child, in adulthood Brigid worked her way to the Christian faith instinctively through kind acts and miracles, from helping the poor to turning water into beer. But she was unique: she refused to marry, asking God to pluck out her eyes to tarnish her beauty (although they reappeared when she 'took the veil'). She fell asleep in sermons and was once ordained – accidentally – as a bishop. She founded communal worship for women, the Kildare monastery, an art school and a smithing school, and inspired an eternal flame protected by a man-proof hedge that would induce madness in any male who crossed it. Brigid is also an accidental lesbian icon: she had a female 'soul friend' and bedfellow, Darlughdach, who became the abbess of Kildare after Brigid's death and died one year to the day after her mentor.

Around 650 CE, a monk, Cogitosus of Kildare, wrote a biography of Brigid's life, just 75 years or so after she is said to have died. In recent years, his *Vita Sanctae Brigidae* has become a hugely controversial text for his depiction of Brigid helping a young woman who had accidentally become pregnant. 'Brigid, exercising with the most strength of her ineffable faith,' writes Cogitosus, 'blessed her, caused the foetus to disappear without coming to birth, and without pain.' Was this the first recorded saint-sanctified abortion? Pro-choice advocates in Ireland have invoked her in recent years, drawing on her power in the abortion debate; and Brigid's image and name pops up in discussions surrounding sexual health, abortion centres and pro-choice activism.

In Haitian Vodou culture, Brigid has her third incarnation as Maman Brigitte. Retaining the red hair and pale face of pagan Brigid and Saint Brigid of Kildare, Maman is a lwa death spirit who drinks spicy rum and loves to swear. Haitian Vodou is influenced by the forced diaspora of enslaved people from Haiti and the Americas and has a rich ideological system of deities, rituals and ceremonies, with incredible diversity of belief. Maman Brigitte is thought to be syncretized (whereby different cultural beliefs and stories intertwine) with both Brigid's pagan and Christian personas. But much like the pagan and Christian versions, Maman Brigitte is a deity in her own right. Like many of the lwa spirits, she is ancient, fizzing with female power, and holds a special place in Louisiana Voodoo. Established in 1990, the Voodoo Spiritual Temple in New Orleans celebrates traditional West African spirituality and culture, herbal healing and ceremonies. These rites and rituals continue to connect temple-goers with the power of deities like Maman Brigitte herself; she lives on. Pagan priestess, saintly feminist, potential lesbian, pro-choice advocate and powerful deity of femininity, Brigid is as queer as they come.

THE DJINN
The wish-granting shapeshifters of queer acceptance

The djinn haunt folklore, dreams and nightmares, and the feverish minds of Hollywood showrunners. To some they are malevolent, bringing illness and ill fortune to the innocent; to others they are soothsayers, wish-granters and even lovers. These shapeshifting, and yet often unseen spirits, pre-Islamic and age-old, are hardly heroes of myth and legend, but they have been used as conduits for personal transformation and even queer acceptance.

The main quality of djinn is our inability to pin them down. Competing accounts mire what we know of them, leaving them open to interpretation. Are they the freewheeling spirits of the 'smokeless fire' in ancient Islamic texts; the shedim of Jewish mythology, created from a 'flameless fire'; or the 10 per cent human creatures of Indian folklore? Are they almost-demons or nearly angelic? Or perhaps they are the evil

unseen force in Babak Anvari's Persian-language horror movie *Under the Shadow* (2016) or Robin Williams's rambunctious bright-blue chatterbox in Disney's *Aladdin* (1992)?

One thing the old stories seem to agree on is that djinn have free will – they can be as manipulative or as helpful as they please. They can bring sickness, grant wishes, tell the future or even turn into snakes, and they have their own queer-edged devotees. In Classical Arabic, the Mukhannath, or 'effeminate ones', were a male-bodied, possibly gay community who existed in a sort of gender hinterland. In ancient times they might be celebrated singers or performers, wander the lands, or safely serve wealthy women because of their apparent 'lack of desire', which has led modern historians to place them firmly in the Q for Queer file. But they also are associated with the djinn and thought, by some, to be their servants (although linking queer people with demonic forces seems like an easy win for the ancient ones).

In modern times, writers have used the Djinn as a stand-in for gayness. In Tofik Dibi's coming-out memoir *Djinn* (2015), he recounts his time in the Dutch parliament as a young firebrand fighting for Muslim equality but also secretly struggling with his sexuality. For Dibi, the Djinn was the internal voice that held him down, the entity that shadowed his every moment. In his memoir, Dibi even asks family members about the ancient rites and rituals that might purge the djinn from his body. Eventually he grows to accept his true nature, and the djinn that never was is finally no more.

In the Starz TV series *American Gods* (2017–21), adapted from Neil Gaiman's beloved fantasy novel of the same name, the djinn arrives full-bodied and full-blooded on screen. During a battle between the old gods and the new, a cast of ancient and contemporary creations fight, eat humans and get it on. And in New York City, a shy Omani salesman, Salim (played by Omid Abtahi), who half-heartedly sells souvenirs to appease his family back home, encounters Mousa Kraish's taxi driver, a fiery djinn with one thing on his mind. There is folklore that suggests djinn got it on with humans and the pair soon decamp to a seedy motel room and do what djinn and humans do naturally: have passionate, hairy-chested butt sex.

As Kraish's djinn emerges from the bathroom, glistening wet, his eyes burn in the dark and his towel drops to the floor. What follows is a sex scene, complete with CGI penises, that gay showrunner Bryan Fuller – and co-showrunner Michael Green – wanted to be as passionate and as realistic as possible, expanding on Gaiman's original scene in the novel. It did not come easily, as they say, with Fuller advising a reshoot when the male–male sexual mechanics went awry: '. . . you guys need to go back and figure where holes are,' he recounted in an interview with Josh Wigler for *The Hollywood Reporter* in 2017. 'We wanted it to be real,' Kraish has said of the same scene, 'and we both wanted it to be about two men who are in love with one another.' As the pair spend one sweaty night together, their skin darkens and the djinn's eyes continue to burn.

Both Gaiman's version of the djinn and the steamy TV adaptation seem to answer Salim's longing for queer acceptance. In among the thrusts, the djinn – who claims not to grant wishes – gives Salim the affection, tenderness and validation he craves, something he has never experienced before. 'We felt like the djinn, in this romantic gesture, wanted to give him a more intimate sexual experience,' explained Fuller. In the end, Salim wakes to find that the djinn has disappeared with all his things, even his salesman's suit. He resolves to dress in the djinn's clothes instead, take his ID and even drive his taxi. Salim effectively becomes the djinn himself, escaping the oppressive life he hates in Oman.

This seems to be the true queer gift of the djinn: they might haunt your dreams, turn into a snake or steal your clothes, but they always bring about some sort of unexpected transformation, and often for the better. 'I do not grant wishes,' says the naked, musclebound onscreen djinn of *American Gods*. Gazing up at him in wonder, as if he is all he ever wanted, Salim simply replies: 'But you do.'

SHIKHANDI

The gender-nonconforming, sex-changing warrior queen

Meet Shikhandi, fearless warrior, one of the scene-stealers of the *Mahābhārata* – the legendary Ancient Indian Sanskrit epic – and proud gender nonconformist. In the immense *Mahābhārata* lies 1.8 million words and 200,000 verse lines of stories, devotional Hindu and philosophical passages, the holy Bhagavad Gita and the rambling story of the Kurukshetra War and its generations of warring cousins. Shikhandi is one of its minor stars, an androgynous young royal who – depending on which version of the story you read – magically changes their sex or gender, or bravely breaks the rules as a female who lives as a man.

The *Mahābhārata* first tells of another character, Princess Amba, who dies before she can seek revenge against her kidnapper, Bhishma. The deity Shiva appears to console her, telling her that she will help cause his death in the next life, and soon after she is reincarnated as Shikhandi – it's complicated. But in her *Indian Tales of the Great Ones* (1916), Cornelia Sorabji gives 'The Story of the Maiden-Knight' a pared-down, Disney-like spin. In Sorabji's version, a fairy-tale king and queen are desperate to conceive, and Shiva answers their prayers, only in a mystifying way. They will be blessed with a son, says Shiva, who should first be a daughter. Without quibbling, when their child is born, they name them Shikhandi and although the child is a 'daughter', according to Sorabji, the queen insists 'she is a son' and raises Shikhandi as such.

Their child grows to be strong and fair and soon is of marrying age. A suitable princess is found but Shikhandi's femaleness is discovered, the princess's father threatens war and Shikhandi runs away. Shortly after Shikhandi encounters a male yaksha, a nature spirit called Sthuna, and cries out: ' "Make me a man,' said she, "a perfect man." ' Granting their wish, Sthuna swaps bodies with Shikhandi, saving their father. 'So was fulfilled the promise of Shiva,' writes Sorabji. ' "She shall be first a daughter: and then a son, Shikhandi, Maiden-Knight." '

In Ruth Vanita and Saleem Kidwai's *Same-Sex Love in India* (2000), Vanita is clear that something extraordinary happens to the character. 'The story of Shikhandi is perhaps the best-known case of sex change in any Ancient Indian text,' writes Vanita. She points out that 'Shikhandi' later became a term to refer to 'men of doubtful sexuality' (read: gay). But for Vanita, the myth is fascinating due to its 'sex change-rebirth, the cross-dressed girl-child married to another girl, her desire to be a man, and' – considering all the competing versions of the story – 'the uncertainty regarding the permanence of the change.'

In recent times, other writers have also re-examined the Shikhandi tale through a queer lens. In Devdutt Patanaik's *Shikhandi And Other Tales They Don't Tell You* (2014) he unpicks popular old myths to unearth their queer elements. His take on the legend is simple: Shikhandi became a man to satisfy their new wife. In his version, Sthuna lends Shikhandi his manhood for just one night – the wedding night – and they change sex to fulfil the duties expected of a new husband. And in *Slumdog Millionaire* actor Faezeh Jalali's comic play *Shikhandi: The Story of the In-Betweens* (2017), she places the story in contemporary times: 'When Shikhandi tries to tell Dhrupad, his father, about his gender confusion, the latter immediately suggests marriage as a solution,' she said in an interview with Srinivasan Avi in *The Hindu* in 2018. 'That is exactly how parents and family react when a person declares [themselves] to be gay or lesbian.'

Although LGBTQ+ people have limited rights in India, one group, the hijra, still face almost complete marginalization. The hijra community is as old as the ancient texts, a community of low-status, gender-nonconforming and femme-presenting people who are forced to live on the sidelines of society and almost always in poverty. Although the legend of Shikhandi is thought to show Hindu acknowledgement of trans people, it is of little use to them. But what these new takes on old *Mahābhārata* myths show is that changing sex – or being gender nonconforming – is not particularly novel or Western-centric. Perhaps being a butch female or a femme male, or being trans, has deep roots in ancient storytelling?

ORLANDO

Woolf's immortal queer hero inspired by real-life love

In 1928, literary lesbian Virginia Woolf (1882–1941) published her novel *Orlando: A Biography*. The fantastical tale follows a young and sweetly oblivious Elizabethan boy-poet who travels agelessly through centuries of English history from the court of Elizabeth I – where he is the queen's favourite – to Constantinople. In between is ice-skating on the Thames River, a torrid love affair with a Russian princess, and an unexplained change of sex, after which Lady Orlando goes on to live for 300 years, dressing alternately as a man or woman, and marries a gender-nonconforming sea captain. Put simply, *Orlando* is a queer mythical work with major feminist, lesbian and trans vibes.

The character – and the novel itself – is a love letter to the object of Woolf's affection, the celebrated bisexual author Vita Sackville-West. The pair were literary contemporaries, and

Woolf was in awe of Sackville-West; she certainly struggled to keep up with the baroness's 35 books – including eight full-length novels and five plays before she turned 18 – and had to make do with being only one of Vita's female lovers. Drawing from Vita's incredible life, Woolf was particularly fascinated by Sackville-West's male persona, Julian. He would make appearances, suited and booted, at small gatherings and at one memorable trip to Monte Carlo with her then lover, Violet Trefusis, before both were dragged home by their husbands. But the attraction wasn't one-sided: for Vita, a feverish sapiosexual, Woolf was the perfect intellectual counterpart. They sent each other love letters, shared gossip and wandered the Sackville-West's famous garden; Vita even gifted Virginia one of her own Cocker Spaniel puppies. It was true lesbian love.

Orlando is directly connected to Vita, a hymn to her freewheeling life of writing, social commentary and getting it on with whomever she fancied regardless of gender, age, place or marital status. Woolf gives Vita's male alter ego, Julian, an Elizabethan makeover, a sex makeover and then a gender makeover – Orlando was queer before Queer Theory was a twinkle in the eye of Foucault fan scholars of the 1990s. Other characters in Woolf and Sackville-West's lives also crept into the novel: the rough-edged Princess Sasha, with whom Orlando has an ill-fated love affair, is thought to be Violet, Vita's onetime lover. (Violet responded in 1939 with her own take-down novel, *Broderie Anglaise*, belittling Vita and Virginia's relationship. Revenge is a dish best served published, as a novel.)

Nearly seven decades later, in 1992, Orlando transformed again, only this time through the lens of filmmaker Sally Potter. In Potter's gorgeously camp cinematic version, Tilda Swinton plays Orlando, a thoughtful yet childlike 400-year-old goof who is still alive at the time of the film's release. Swinton is androgynous and measured, and painfully cool, breaking down the fourth wall with knowing glances to the camera. The film was something of a queer turning point; it signified a cultural moment, with its cameos from late, great gay icon Quentin Crisp as a decrepit Queen Elizabeth I, and Jimmy Sommerville as a falsetto cherub singing '. . . neither a woman nor a man'. And it pointed a new generation of queer-literate readers to Woolf's original novel.

Since then, queer people and others have returned again and again to both Potter's film and Woolf's original text. The latter is particularly important to queer cartoonist Alison Bechdel, author of the weekly comic strip *Dykes to Watch Out For* (1983–2008) and the autobiographical graphic memoir *Fun Home: A Family Tragicomic* (2006). 'It's hard to fathom how Virginia could play so freely with sexual identity in that much more conservative era,' she writes in the introduction to the book *Love Letters: Vita and Virginia* by Virginia Woolf and Vita Sackville-West (2021), 'but play she did, inventing her way into the future.' *Oranges Are Not the Only Fruit* author Jeanette Winterson is another *Orlando* afficionado. She points out that, apart from playing around with gender, Woolf uses Orlando's change of sex to highlight sex-based inequality in the 1920s. 'Woolf was preoccupied by the social and economic differences between the sexes,' Winterson wrote in *The Guardian* in 2018, '– differences, she believed, that were gender biases masquerading as facts of life.' In the novel, Orlando marvels at being female but soon becomes mired in the drudge of bureaucratic sexism – and almost loses everything. 'The protagonist spends hundreds of years trying to reclaim his own property and cash,' she writes, 'legally sequestered after he wakes up as a woman.'

Inspired by the electrifying life of her female lover, *Orlando* pokes fun at Woolf's love rivals and the sexism of the 1920s while celebrating Sackville-West's male persona, allowing Orlando to be reborn, changing their sex with a few clunks of her typewriter. In this way, Woolf creates a contemporary queer myth, bringing together feminism, clever satire and fantastical genderplay. She expects us to accept Orlando, our hero, whichever sex they are. In Potter's film, she quietly does the same: when Lady Orlando arrives home from Constantinople – after leaving a decade before, as Lord Orlando – she meets her old staff at the door. 'Well, here I am again!' she says, mentioning nothing of her obvious change of sex. Her servants merely glance at each other, smile, and get on with things.

THE DAUGHTERS OF BILITIS

The secret lesbian society of feminists who loved to dance

Most mythical tales stretch back through the aeons, rooted in ancient gods, monsters and magic – but not all. Some have more modern origins but have just the same fantastical, inspirational and transformative appeal. Meet the Daughters of Bilitis, a secret band of Sappho-inspired warrior women who had two things in common: they were lesbians who loved to dance – and they went on to change the world.

In 1950s San Francisco lived Rose Bamberger, a young Filipina woman, and Rosemary Sliepen, her white girlfriend. Although the city had a thriving underground queer scene, nightclubs, bars and queer hangouts were on the down-low – police would raid gay and lesbian establishments and rough up patrons, sometimes posing as gay men and lesbians to entrap their prey. And the joy of same-sex dancing? Out of the question. Rose had an idea and, with Rosemary, reached out to a tiny group of fellow lesbians with the aim of setting up a secret society – not least so that they could dance without fear in each other's homes.

The name was something of a code, an obscure in-joke that Rose and Rosemary hoped would pique the interest of fellow lesbians only. Bilitis was thought to have been a lover of ancient lesbian icon Sappho (see page 43), and a translation of her steamy verse by French poet Pierre Louÿs was published in 1955. *The Songs of Bilitis* had set the literary and lesbian worlds alight with its girl-on-girl eroticism (until it was discovered that Louÿs had probably made the whole thing up). Rose and Rosemary founded their lesbian social club Daughters of Bilitis that same year. They soon had a small but loyal following and an application card with the motto 'Que Viva' ('On the alert').

Original members Del Martin and Phyllis Lyon, a couple, are credited with giving Daughters of Bilitis its activist slant. This initially caused friction in the group: Rose, being Filipina, and other working-class members of DOB had more to lose – they wanted the group to stay social but secret. But Del and Phyllis, two journalism grads living on Castro Street, wanted more. 'It was so scary,' admits Phyllis on Eric Marcus's *Making Gay History* podcast (from an interview recorded in 1989). 'There was nothing but fear out there,' Del added. Lesbians were fearful of 'losing their jobs, losing their families, losing their minds,' Phyllis continued; 'a lot of women came to DOB who had been either abandoned by their families or had [...] had electroshock therapy, or. . . had escaped from mental institutions.'

Del and Phyllis's fears were realized when the FBI, which had apparently infiltrated the group, reported on a DOB breakfast event in the late 1950s ('Big deal!' Phyllis guffaws in Marcus's interview). The Daughters were undeterred; Del became president and Phyllis club secretary, and membership grew. The Daughters published their newsletter, *The Ladder*, the year after they were founded, reaching thousands of mail subscribers at its peak. And by 1959 the group had proudly officiated local chapters in New York, Rhode Island, Chicago and Los Angeles, and held conferences well into the 1960s. Along with creating a refuge, a place to have fun and come out, the Daughters helped transform how wider society perceived lesbians, bravely raising visibility and challenging misconceptions.

The group fractured in the mid- to late 1960s, with some Daughters wondering whether the group should continue to focus on gay rights or fight the patriarchy for all women. An editor of *The Ladder* was controversially removed from her role after inviting male writers to contribute; some Daughters joined other gay-rights groups; and Del and Phyllis started working more closely with the National Organization for Women. And in 1970 *The Ladder* was taken over by a new faction who abhorred its lesbian-only remit. It closed two years later, and by 1978 the Daughters of Bilitis was no more.

Decades on, the group now has mythical status. Inspired by a young woman of colour, its leaders lauded as queer heroes for going against the grain of society, the Daughters of Bilitis bravely carved out a space for lesbians – first in the safety of each other's homes and then, as queer acceptance grew, audaciously out in public. Their enduring legacy is simple yet powerful and just as relevant today as it was back in 1955: 'You know, we were trying to help lesbians find themselves . . .' said Phyllis, 'I mean, you can't have a movement if you don't have people that see that they're worthwhile.'

SEDNA

Woman of the waves and eternally wronged daughter of Inuit folklore

Woman of the Waves, Mother of the Deep, or simply Big Bad Woman, Sedna – also known as Sana, or Sanna – is the mysterious fingerless Inuit outcast who rules the icy waters of the underworld. To many, she is the vengeful spirit of the Arctic, withholding the fruits of the ocean from those who depend on it; to others she is a queer hero who, wronged by her family, rightfully seeks her revenge. Although the myth changes from community to community, Sedna has inspired countless pieces of ancient and contemporary art, literature and stories that are part of the Inuit cultural universe.

Canadian writer and Inuit folklorist Rachel Attituq Qitsualik-Tinsley's version of the story is a masterclass in icy betrayal, transformation and quiet revenge. In her series of pieces for *Nunatsiaq News* (1999), she tells of a gnarly-faced tuurngak, a malevolent bird-spirit who, wearing a disguise, tricks wilful and 'finicky' Sedna into marriage and takes her to the worst starter-home ever: 'a blackened hut that squatted like some fetid carcass among numerous piles of ancient bones and refuse'.

When Sedna's parents try to enact her rescue with the help of a boatload of musclebound youths, the bird-spirit threatens to kill them all. Her parents watch from the shore, aghast as the youths, fearing for their own lives, push Sedna overboard and whack at her hands with their oars as she grips onto the side – until her fingers are gone. As she slowly slips into the icy water 'her father met her gaze . . . seeing that her eyes reflected not fear any longer, but only the wisdom that comes with disillusionment and betrayal'. From her fingers grow seals, whales and walruses – the sea life that many early Inuit would depend on for their survival.

In many versions of the myth, much is made of Sedna's refusal of her male suitors and eventual gross-out at her husband, but what Qitsualik-Tinsley calls 'finicky' others might see as queer. The trope of a young gay person battling the pressures of heteronormativity and stepping over the gender boundary only to be punished and then transformed is a strong one. In all the Sedna or Sanna stories, there is tension between her and her father, and she is sacrificed to the sea. But in some she is both male and female, and even takes a female lover in the underworld. Eventually she becomes 'the fingerless, lice-ridden hag beneath the sea – mistress of marine mammals', writes Qitsualik-Tinsley. The idea of the 'hag' is important here: Sedna is an ostracized woman, too old, too ugly, too difficult, refusing to conform. Women like Sedna haunt the myths and ancient stories of many cultures, marking women out as unknowable, untamed and incongruous within the patriarchy. Simply, they are very, very queer indeed.

The story of a powerful female Inuit being is at odds with much of outsider writing about Inuit nations. It was once thought that women played a subservient role in early Inuit communities, but many claim that before European contact – the arrival of male whalers, traders, explorers and such – this was not the case. Was Sedna a powerful deity, a superbeing from dark, icy waters, or a benevolent creator – a mother figure – who brought richness of life to the sea, the Inuit's main source of food and survival? 'She is not a goddess,' confirms Qitsualik-Tinsley, 'but rather a special creature of fear and tragedy.'

In the 2014 play *War Lesbian*, experimental theatre-maker Haruna Lee and their onetime theatre company harunalee drew on the Sedna legend, reimagining it as a scrappy, comic and very queer tale. With the cast writhing around in crushed-paper snow, Sedna – a young Alaskan gal – devours her arctic bro boyfriend, finds lesbian love under the sea and encounters her true vibe as a warmonger, overseen by a demonic Ellen DeGeneres (played by Lee themselves), all to a peppy show-tune score. In *War Lesbian*, Sedna's girlfriend is the character Qualertetang, another female mythic being drawn from the Inuit stories and often thought to be Sedna's ocean-dwelling love interest.

War Lesbian isn't the only contemporary, offbeat interpretation of the Sedna myth. In the contemporary world of gong baths, crystals and online covens, Sedna and Qualertetang live on. They can be called upon in *The Craft*-style queer spell-casting ceremonies, complete with merch, from shamanic amulets and devotionals to a Sedna Goddess Empowerment Kit. Whoever she was – wronged girl turned vengeful outcast, 'special creature of fear', or queer hero refusing the tidal wave of heteronormative pressure – Sedna endures in the icy depths of myth, legend and Etsy.

LESTAT AND LOUIS

Literature's first-ever vampire same-sex parents

Delightfully camp yet deathly evil, Lestat de Lioncourt is the immortal party boy, all frilly cuffs and charisma, with an insatiable thirst for blood and trouble, and is arguably fiction's second-most notorious vampire (after Dracula himself). The late Anne Rice's much-loved debut novel *Interview with the Vampire* (1976) charts his centuries-long love affair with mournful male beauty Louis de Pointe du Lac, the raven-haired nihilist and vampire, and the couple's decades with Claudia, a fellow creature of darkness, forever five years old. Louis narrates his life to a writer in modern-day San Francisco, a tall tale of 1790s colonial New Orleans and the old world of Europe, in which Lestat and Louis's toxic relationship weathers poisonings, embarrassing costume changes, snippy put-downs and murder by sunlight. And for years, especially in the realms of horror forums, fanfic and fan-art sites (where

Lestat and Louis have a new life as bulging, muscly male lovers), the pair have become nothing less than mythical.

On its release, critics merely shrugged at Rice's debut, but readers adored it. *Interview* became a bestseller, igniting a cultural obsession with vampires, and the author worked on expanding her bloody universe, publishing a string of other modern Gothic novels over the decades, including steamy non-vampiric erotica. But what was most fascinating about *Interview* and its follow-ups was the inherent queerness of Lestat and Louis, who are, for all intents and purposes, a bisexual male couple.

Much has been written about the erotic nature of the vampire world. Vampires – strong, beautiful, deadly – are monsters who seem to threaten sexual dominion but in fact go even further, literally sucking the life out of their prey. These scenes, in Rice's book and in Neil Jordan's 1994 film adaptation, lock Lestat and Louis in a barely concealed act of intimacy, with reluctant Louis eventually giving himself over to Lestat's chaotic top energy. After Lestat sucks Louis and the pair have exchanged bodily fluids, Louis is transformed and, apart from magical powers and immortality, has gained a new perspective. Lestat has him thoroughly and utterly queered – and gasping for more.

Rice drew on her childhood in New Orleans, her Roman Catholic upbringing and her love of vampire movies to inform

Interview, but she was also influenced by her mother's death when she was just 15 and, later, her time in the sex-positive Haight-Ashbury of the 1960s where she was happy to be a 'square' in a community of anything but. In 1988 she told *The New York Times* (more than a decade after the paper had rolled its eyes at her debut) how important *Interview* was for her: 'For the first time, I was able to describe my reality, the dark, Gothic influence on my childhood,' she said. 'It's not fantasy for me. My childhood came to life . . .' And more besides: vampire-child Claudia is an echo of Michele, Rice's daughter, who tragically died aged five.

In the film, Tom Cruise gives full wattage to Lestat's acidic campness, and Brad Pitt is spellbindingly beautiful and sad as Louis. Although the actors don't play their characters as explicitly gay, there is little doubt they are a male couple – though on the film's release most audiences missed the work's queer coding. Even so, Rice worried that the story's gay subtext would spook the film studios. A gay blockbuster was unheard of, and she even considered rewriting the story so that Cher could play Louis's character (which would, of course, have made it even queerer). In the end, Lestat and Louis endured as a male couple, their queerness hidden in plain sight.

There is another way in which Lestat and Louis might be considered bisexual or gay. In both the novel and film, the addition of Claudia completes the trio, until she is murdered by a jealous Lestat. In 2012, when Rice was 71 years young, it was pointed out to her that, in modern times, Lestat and Louis might be considered Claudia's parents. She laughed and said, 'Sure! I never thought of it, they were the first vampire same-sex parents.'

Lestat and Louis live on across all the works in Rice's *Vampire Chronicles*, the enduring love of the film, and countless fan contributions and Comic-Con cosplay dress-ups where new generations of *Interview*-lovers celebrate the queer vampire couple with frilly cuffs and fangs. All this and the ANC *Interview* TV series (where Louis is now the subject of a podcast) proves that there's queer life in the undead yet.

THE SACRED BAND OF THEBES

The elite army corps of merciless male lovers

In 1993, after decades of banning gay and lesbian servicemen and women, the US military took a tentative first step in finally acknowledging its queer personnel. President Clinton's 'Don't ask, don't tell' (DADT) policy was a compromise meant to appease military traditionalists worried more about any potential shower-room antics than the life and death of their soldiers. Although DADT allowed gay, lesbian and bisexual people to serve, it was a promise to ignore the lived realities of thousands of soldiers, sailors, air-force crew and their support staff who were ready to lay down their lives for their country. A form of DADT was active until 2011 when President Obama repealed the ban, with trans personnel gaining access in 2016. But the US military is by no means the world's first fighting force to accept queer people. More than 2,000 years before, another troop dominated the world of Ancient Greece – an elite corps that appeared to rely on, and celebrate, the sexuality of its soldiers.

To the city of Thebes, one of the oldest Greek cities and the mythical birthplace of Dionysus and Heracles. At the centre of the most fertile land in the region, Thebes was the envy of Greece, and its citizens were wealthy, powerful and almost always under attack. Having made and broken numerous military alliances over the centuries, early in the 3rd century BCE Thebans found themselves under the influence of neighbouring Sparta. A resistance formed that sought to overthrow the regime so as to claim freedom and democracy for the people. This rabble of militia men was no match for the Spartans' military prowess, but the Thebans had an idea: they would create a standing unit of 300 soldiers, train them to be merciless killing machines and get them to lead the army.

It was war hero Gorgidas who put together the squad known as the Sacred Band of Thebes, with the famous Pelopidas taking over soon after. In their first skirmish with the Spartans, the Battle of Leuctra in 371 BCE, they were outnumbered, and defeat looked inevitable, but the elite corps had a secret weapon: gay power. The infamous Band is thought to have been composed of 150 male couples who not only fought back the Spartans but also won every battle until their demise 40 years later.

'A band that is held together by the friendship between lovers,' writes Greek philosopher and biographer Plutarch in *The Life of Pelopidas* (2nd century CE), 'is . . . not to be broken, since the lovers are ashamed to play the coward before their beloved, and the beloved before their lovers, and both stand firm in danger to protect each other.' Plutarch, our main source of the Sacred Band's gay make-up, claimed it is precisely that these men were lovers that gave them an edge on the battlefield. Their love and desire for one another made them stronger fighters – each being willing to fight to the death because of their relationship, to protect the man he loved.

Some have cast doubt on Plutarch's account. He is the sole source of the Sacred Band of Boyfriends' membership policy and wrote almost 500 years after its demise. Was the Band not just older Theban elites and their handpicked favourites? Perhaps Plutarch was under the influence of Thebes' mythical relationship with Heracles, who Plutarch also claimed had a string of male conquests under his godly tunic?

But it seems that Pelopidas, the leader of the Sacred Band, was in thrall to Plato's notion of 'eros', the idea that love was the strongest foundation that could unite a group. To Plato, eros was a sort of energy, a passion that could be harnessed and diverted into all manner of things, from philosophy to art to bonds between men. To Plato, this eros-inspired relationship – intertwined with sexuality, although not necessarily sexual – is the ideal, and Pelopidas thought so too. But there is something problematic here: perhaps Pelopidas abused the soldiers' mutual affections, weaponizing the fact that each man might be willing to die for his partner. After 40 years, the Sacred Band's final fight with the army of Philip II of Macedon ended in catastrophic failure. In 338 BCE, every Sacred Band couple perished in the bloody Battle of Chaeronea; according to Plutarch, their bodies lay entwined with each other, with a regretful Philip weeping over them.

More than 2,000 years later, in 1818, young British architect George Ledwell Taylor and his friends were summering in Greece when they stumbled upon the remains of what seemed to be the Lion of Chaeronea, a huge marble monument thought to have been erected to commemorate the fall of the Sacred Band. In its pedestal were buried spears and shields with the men's names engraved; later still, the skeletons of 254 men were uncovered by archaeologists. In 1902, a secret British gay society, the Order of Chaeronea, helped fund the Lion's restoration. It stands there still, 20 feet tall, overlooking the now empty graves of the Sacred Band of Thebes, men who gave their lives for one another, bonded by love.

THE ORDER OF CHAERONEA

The secret gay activists of the early 1900s

In 1893, British poet George Cecil Ives (1867–1950) had had enough. A member of the Humanitarian League, a radical group campaigning for human rights, Ives was well versed in activism, bravely pushing for improved treatment of gay men, something he called 'the Cause'. But it wasn't enough: he saw how gay men had yet to win even begrudging acceptance in wider society, and faced state-sanctioned abuse, ostracization and even imprisonment. Openly organizing was near-impossible but Ives was undeterred; he devised an underground means of communication, uniting a selected few of influence and power via a secret gay society. In 1897 the Order of Chaeronea was born, a political organization of foppish, upper-class gay men who looked back to the classical world to understand their place in the present. The order was inspired by the fall of the Sacred Band of Thebes, the merciless elite army corps of possibly male lovers who perished at the Battle of Chaeronea in 338 BCE (see page 137). Ives hoped that their group might be as powerful as the Sacred Band and go on to change the world.

The Order's founding principles were simple and wonderfully idealistic: 'We believe in the glory of passion / We believe in the inspiration of emotion / We believe in the holiness of love', but the organization was less about flirty socials than creating political influence. That said, Ives imbued the group with an almost religious framework, with rites and rituals, code-speak, an everlasting oath. It was non-hierarchical and members had a way of writing dates that alluded to the Sacred Band of Thebes.

Ives was inspired by his friend, fellow poet and philosopher Edward Carpenter, and by the work of Walt Whitman. He set out to recruit men like his heroes, the brightest and best of the upper-class gay world. But not every man wanted to follow Ives's 'Cause'. Five years before setting up the Order, Ives had been introduced to Oscar Wilde by Lord Alfred Douglas, with whom Ives had had a brief fling. Wilde was instantly attracted to the handsome young Ives, who in turn was entranced by Wilde's story of meeting Whitman on a trip to America. 'I have the kiss of Walt Whitman still on my lip,' Wilde apparently said, as reported in one of Ives's 122 diaries. Both Wilde and Douglas refused to join the Cause; but through them, Ives gained entry to a group of literary A-gays and, although no membership list survives, it is thought that he was able to recruit several of them to the Order. Around 300 gay men and lesbians were members at the Order's peak.

It is worth noting Ives's bravery in founding the Order and attempting to improve life for gay people: he was in his mid-twenties and hundreds of years ahead of his time – he risked so much. Two years before the founding of the Order, Wilde, who had lost an ill-advised libel trial, was imprisoned for having sex with other men, eventually moving to Reading Gaol. Wilde, a seemingly untouchable socialite, was made an example of and his fate sent shockwaves through the gay and lesbian elite, many of whom fled the country. The Order – and its sworn secrecy – became more important than ever.

In 1902, the Order offered to help fund the restoration of a 2,000-year-old monument in Greece, the famous Lion of Chaeronea, that once watched over the graves of the Sacred Band of Thebes (see page 137). The monument stands to this day, and Ives's own diaries (some written in code) and 45 scrapbooks have also survived. They give his account of the upper-class world of gay writers and aesthetes of the late 1800s and beyond, including his impressions of Wilde, Douglas and others plus musings about drag, parties and even cricket (but let's not hold that against him). Little is known about the actions of the group, but its members' high position in society, along with their aim to improve life for gay men and lesbians, would have made them an influential if subtle force. Fascinatingly, Ives's Order – in a new, modern form – seems to still be active. Their mysterious movements online means that the group are thought of by some as a gay Illuminati, their membership still shrouded in secrecy.

ILA AND BUDHA

The genderflux star of the *Mahābhārata* and their demigod husband

Ancient Sanskrit epics the *Mahābhārata* and *Ramayana* – and the religious Puranas, a vast collection of Indian writing – are considered the lodestones of Hinduism, one of the world's oldest surviving religions. In among feuding royals, deathly curses, a world-creating cosmic serpent, ape men and warrior women is a cast of glittering gods and mortals who fall in and out of love, fight in wars, have affairs, live lives of bravery and valour – and change sex. Woven around the philosophical and devotional verse are fantastical tales of eternal transformation, and one rather queer story of mythical power.

Meet Ila, also known as Sudyumna, a genderflux hero and creator of the Lunar dynasty of Indian kings. The eldest child of the cosmic megabeing Vaivasvata Manu, Ila is at times a woman, at times a man: they are born female (as Ila) and transform magically to male (Sudyumna). Being genderflux is Ila's superpower, passed to them in the form of a curse after they mistakenly wander the sacred grove of the goddess Parvati, after which Ila flits between the two binaries of the story.

All the myths point to Ila being born female, but in some versions their parents were desperate for a boy (a gender trope in many ancient myths) and this desire was answered with a touch of magic. King Ila looms large in the texts, with competing stories charting a fascinating life, with them first transgressing Parvati's grove, Sharavana, in which all male mortals are transformed into females. In fact, in the *Bhagavata Purana* Ila's entire crew enjoy the same magical conversion. Parvati took pity on the freshly female Ila and allowed them to transition month-to-month between the genders; but when Ila was female they would not remember their previous month as male, and vice versa.

One day, in their female form, Ila caught the eye of Budha, son of the moon god. Budha had been practising abstinence, but seeing Ila changed all that; he was smitten. The pair married and spent a month together before Ila turned male again. Little is written about Budha's reaction to Ila's magical monthly transformation, but it seems that Ila would spend those weeks learning piety and doing spiritual tasks for their husband – and presumably grooming their beard. After nine months, Ila gave birth and the Lunar dynasty began.

Eventually, more magic creeps into the story (peculiarly, a horse is involved) and Ila becomes permanently male.

The fantastical story of Ila and Budha is not obscure marginalia but remains an integral part of the ancient texts. Yet, as with Shikhandi, the gender-nonconforming warrior (see page 115), contemporary Indian culture – forward-thinking but steeped in myth – seems to have all but forgotten Ila's genderflux state. Ila's story seems to have had little effect on modern Indian attitudes and the treatment of trans people in India, for whom Ila might be a sort of ideological forerunner, is hardly befitting the mother of the Lunar dynasty. The hijra, an Indian trans-femme group sometimes described as the 'third gender' and numbering in the millions, has lived mainly in poverty for centuries. Only recently have some of them attained basic security, and some hijra are slowly being recognized as trans women. But if Ila – such an important figure in Hindu mythology – might be considered a sort of ancestor to gender-diverse people in India, her transformative powers seem to have been broadly ignored.

BUDÛR AND QAMAR

The unlikely queer-edged lovers of
One Thousand and One Nights

The glittering jewel of the Islamic Golden Age, *Alf laylah wa laylah*, is a vast collection of Middle Eastern folk tales that entered the Western consciousness in 1702 via Antoine Galland's French translation. In the Western world, it is more commonly known as *One Thousand and One Nights*, and 18th-century readers were delighted and more than a little titillated with its politely naughty goings-on.

The stories, some linking back to ancient times, feature a cast of characters and story structures that have become integral to modern writing, from the classics to contemporary detective and horror archetypes. Some are transgressive, some hilarious, some both: 'Abu Hasan and the Fart' is the tale of a man so humiliated by letting rip at his own wedding that he runs away, only to return a decade later to discover that his fart has not been forgotten but is now famous and appears on the calendar to date other events. *One Thousand and One Nights* also inspired legendary gay filmmaker Pier Paolo Pasolini's *Arabian Nights* (1974), a subtly queer-edged film full of 1970s naked cavorting, many bare bums and a phallic bow and arrow (a nod to some steamy erotic art from 17th-century Rajput).

But if Aladdin, Ali Baba and his 40 thieves, Scheherazade and Sinbad are the megastars of *One Thousand and One Nights*, then there are some eyebrow-raising, cross-dressing genderplayers in between. Roles are reversed, tradition is thrown out the window and same-sex funny business is almost always on the cards. Take the story of the powerful Princess Budûr and her lover Prince Qamar, who – after reluctantly falling in love – are separated, leaving Budûr alone and in crisis. That is, until she dresses up as Prince Qamar and enjoys all his male entitlements, even marrying her own princess and becoming a king before he shows up again. And when he does, Budûr soon leads him to bed; except that Qumar thinks he is being bedded by another man – a king, no less – and shrieks, 'I am not very good at this,' in a nervous retort.

Then there is Zumurrud and her male lover Alî Shâr. The pair are separated when Zumurrud is kidnapped, but she dresses as a man and escapes, eventually becoming king. Later, King Zumurrud has the chance to execute her kidnapper (which she does, of course) before reuniting with Alî Shâr and, um, testing his boundaries in bed.

In Frank G Bosman's essay 'I Am Not Very Good at This' (2021) he points out how both couples refuse traditional marriage in some way, and how the stories' main characters are powerful women. There is cross-gender dressing-up, homoerotic play and 'motherly fathers' (the dads of both Budûr and Zumurrud are less patriarchal and more painfully cute). So far, so queer, and even though the stories end with the pairing up of heterosexual couples, the reader has been able to explore a certain queerness along the way, safely hidden behind comic stories themselves: 'both stories are about the joy and excitement of being in a safe environment to experiment with power, sex, gender, and self-identification,' writes Bosman, 'And what a joy it is.'

David Ghanim, in his book *The Sexual World of the Arabian Nights* (2018), points out that many of the stories have a positive outlook on sexuality, with much of the ribald intimacy initiated by women. 'People [in *Alf laylah wa laylah*] accept sexual activities and encounters with ease and enthusiasm,' Ghanim writes. And woah, is it ever sexy. The djinn note Qamar's especially large Aladdin's lamp – and even though Qamar maintains that women do not interest him, and Budûr has no wish to be controlled by a man, when the djinn force them to meet, sparks fly. Budûr goes on to cross-dress and marries a woman; in the end, she keeps her wife and with Qamar forms a sort of power throuple. 'By cross-dressing,' writes Ghanim, 'Budûr gains greater wealth and power, a wife, and a reversed relationship with her husband, albeit provisionally.'

In this way, Budûr is something of a queer hero. She is a woman who avoids heteronormative expectations, plays with gender, enters a same-sex marriage, then a bisexual throuple, and takes control in the bedroom. And Qamar – who similarly tries to dodge his straight responsibilities – ends up in a polyamorous relationship.

Although Budûr ends up married to a man, and presumably goes back to wearing female garb, she has happily flipped a finger to gender boundaries and staked her claim as the queerest woman of the *One Thousand and One Nights*.

THE DOG AND THE SEA

The Gay Ever After fairy tale saved from obscurity

In researching for his digital-animation college degree, Pete Jordi Wood, a UK-based writer and illustrator and author of *Tales from Beyond the Rainbow* (2023), discovered something very, very gay. An old, possibly ancient tale hidden in the folklore books of yore, something that would satisfy his curiosity about the lack of positive LGBTQ+ folk narratives. Hidden in Stith Thompson's iconic *Motif-Index of Folk-Literature* (1932–36) was a pot of gold. After analysing more than 600 stories across Thompson's six volumes, 'I found this weird-ass tale type called "The Dog and the Sea",' Wood told *Forbes* in 2020, 'which existed in multiple languages, but not in English.' Wood went on to translate different European versions of the story in order to uncover the tale itself, and what he found delighted him.

In the tale, an evil yet irresistible sea witch bewitches a tropical nation, turning its people into animals before submerging it under the sea. Later, a poor young sailor, down on his luck, meets a friendly talking dog. They become firm friends; the dog magically grants the sailor wealth and soon leads him on a voyage in which he, as the only one able to resist her wiles, defeats the witch. He frees the people, and restores everyone to their rightful form, with the dog transforming back into a handsome prince. Importantly, the pair end up together. The discovery inspired Wood to write and illustrate several 'Dog and the Sea' projects (including *The Dog and the Sailor*, first published in 2020), leaving a fascinated audience enthralled with the tale's surprisingly happy and very gay ending (Ian McKellen and Russell T Davies are fans).

In recent years, Thompson's folk and fairy tales have been re-examined with a little queer theory in mind, and subtly gay and trans narratives have been uncovered. But not everything could be included in Thompson's anthologies and some stories were left out. That his work would go on to become the major reference point for folkloric stories means that many of these other stories might be no more. But the reason that this tale – unique in that its hero ends up happily ever after with a handsome prince and is, well, pretty gay – was not translated into English is not much of mystery. 'Unfortunately,' Wood told *Forbes*, 'by his own accounts, Stith Thompson brought with him to the editing his own sense of right and wrong.' Gay and lesbian stories and motifs were sometimes filed under 'Unnatural Perversions' or possibly excluded altogether.

Different 'Dog and the Sea' stories have been available in print for more than 100 years, but it is Wood who has rediscovered the tale for English audiences and has helped draw attention to its Gay Ever After ending. 'The witch in it is fabulous,' says Wood, 'and ridiculously beautiful . . .' The sailor's power – that he is the only man who can resist the gorgeous witch's charms – is a queer one. 'There's a bunch of sexual innuendos,' Wood adds. 'Plus the prince is a total dreamboat.'

In many ways, Wood is the perfect custodian of 'The Dog and the Sea': he is gay himself and queer themes have long informed his work, both as an illustrator and screenwriter. His works stand alongside clever and queer reworkings of fairy tales from Emma Donahue's book of short stories *Kissing the Witch* (1997) to Boldizsár M Nagy's *A Fairytale for Everyone* (2020), the Hungarian queer fairy-tale book that Viktor Orban tried to ban, but 'The Dog and the Sea' is not a remix; rather, it's a rediscovery of something that was hidden. It also begs the question: what other queer tales and happy endings have been lost to censorship or exclusion, accidental or otherwise?

ROBIN HOOD

The English folk hero and his band of very Merry Men

The day Robin Hood came out is a day Professor Stephen Knight will never forget. As a world expert on the mythical 13th-century English outlaw and folk hero, Knight set the media world alight with his 1999 paper 'The Forest Queen' and with a tantalizing idea: Robin Hood was gay. The paper, readied for a small Robin Hood conference, focused on the 1849 novel *Maid Marian, Or, The Forest Queen* by Joachim Stocqueler. Knight pointed out, merely as an aside, that Maid Marian had little to do in the story and perhaps the subtitle was a playful nod to theories of Robin's possible gay sexuality.

The response was butt-clenching, with upset academics, urgent interview invites, official statements put out, and Professor Knight caught in the middle. Later that year, he wrote a response, for Boldoutlaw.com, to the furore that had Hood stans all a-quiver. Setting the record straight, as it were, Knight said that the Robin Hood story, 'through all the male bonding, fighting, feasting and intermasculine emotion, can be taken as a saga of homosexual values'.

The Robin Hood of myth is the heroic rebel, fighting against tyranny and capitalistic dictatorship; a skilled archer and swordsman who, with his band of outlaws, would steal from the rich and give to the poor. In some versions of the story, he is the son of a nobleman, fallen from grace. In others he is an everyman figure, a local hero of humble means. But in all versions, he bravely takes on the establishment, outwitting his superiors with skill and prowess, and lives wild in the woods. Over the centuries, he has gained a band of loyal and loving male outlaws and outcasts and a straight love interest in Maid Marian, and has been the subject of countless novels, plays, films and TV shows.

After Knight's paper was published, the simple outlaw tale of Robin Hood, full of moral fibre and male camaraderie, became something quite different. Hood-lovers now had to imagine Robin and his men larking about in the bushes of the 'greenwood', getting into each other's tights and seductively polishing their bows. With Friar Tuck representing the bears, and Will Scarlett the twinks and twunks, Little John now served medieval daddy realness.

Knight wondered why so few journalists had looked deeper into the myth. Was it such a shock to suggest that Robin Hood might be gay, considering the discoveries of 19th-century archivist Joseph Hunter? Hunter had unearthed documents from the 1300s indicating that King Edward II – regarded by many as a gay monarch and described as the 'comely king' in *A Gest of Robin Hood* from the early 16th century – had a personal valet called . . . Robyn Hood. Might he have been the true inspiration behind the myth? Knight suspects others thought the same: in E M Forster's legendary gay novel *Maurice* (1971) the author sees Hood's 'greenwood' as a sort of English queer wonderland where all gay dreams might come true.

There are glimmers of Robin Hood in 14th-century ballads and later in *A Gest of Robin Hood*, the oldest printed document based on the myth. Then came the Victorian novels and then contemporary cinema, from Douglas Fairbanks in *Robin Hood* (1922) and the delightfully camp *The Adventures of Robin Hood* (1938) starring Errol Flynn – all spindly limbs in green tights – to Kevin Costner's 1990s classic *Robin Hood: Prince of Thieves* (1991) with its yacht-rock soundtrack. But few texts explore Robin's queer edge.

Decades later, novelist Robert Rodi (who went on to write for Marvel Comics and DC imprint Vertigo) took Robin to his logical conclusion using Hood's sexual ambivalence as inspiration for *Merry Men* (2018), a queer comic where homosexuality is outlawed and Robin and his men – mostly gay and bi – are very merry indeed. In Rodi's story, Prince John is the anti-gay monarch and Robin and his men are called on to help a local village deal with the tale's villain, the Sheriff of Nottingham. Rodi casts Robin as a 'sexual outlaw rather than a brigand' and suggests that the 'crew in Sherwood Forest were less a band of thieves than a band of lovers'. It makes for surprising and inspiring reading, but also further confuses the issue – just who was Robin Hood? And how merry did he make his men? Rodi lets another Robin Hood expert, Professor Thomas Hahn, have the last word. Hahn's claim that 'Whatever people think Robin Hood is, Robin Hood is,' is the perfect queer-edged description of the hooded man.

VIOLA

Shakespeare's gender-nonconforming hero of *Twelfth Night*

Meet Viola, star of Shakespeare's *Twelfth Night* (1601), and her twin Sebastian, two shipwreck survivors who each believes the other drowned. On the shores of a new kingdom, Viola quickly disguises herself as a man, creating the male persona Cesario, and gets a job with Duke Orsino. One of Viola/Cesario's first tasks is to deliver a love letter to Orsino's crush, Olivia, only the plan backfires and Olivia falls in love with Cesario instead – unaware that the object of her affection is not a handsome young buck but Viola, a female in disguise. If that is not complicated enough, Viola has a crush of her own: Orsino. Oh, and then Sebastian reappears and Olivia mistakes him for her love, Cesario. It's all one big, fascinating, gender-bending mess and its dramatic unpicking has delighted audiences for hundreds of years.

Shakespeare loved to trick his audience, disguising characters and having them transform on stage. The play was

thought to have been first performed for a Christmas pageant with the real Duke Orsino himself in the attendance; and *Twelfth Night*'s original Elizabethan audiences would have had their heads turned inside out at the spectacle. Even though England had long had a female monarch, theatre was a strictly male domain, with young men and boys playing Shakespeare's female roles. Delightful gender-bender Viola would have been played by a man, playing a woman, playing a man. 'The effects of this casting should not be underestimated,' writes Miranda Fay Thomas in her essay 'A Queer Reading of *Twelfth Night*' (2016); '. . . it would have inevitably lent an extra frisson to the heterosexual relationships portrayed onstage, which would only be further enhanced by a play like *Twelfth Night*.' For all its sweetly comedic confusions, *Twelfth Night* supercharges gender, overloading our expectations and short-circuiting our heteronormative brains.

Like many old and ancient stories, *Twelfth Night* uses comedy, confusion and an 'all's well that ends well' conclusion to create a safe space to play with gender; a fantasy land where anything goes. In another story, Viola might well be the antagonist, transgressing sacred boundaries as a gender troublemaker, but in *Twelfth Night* she is allowed to be the hero, propped up by hilarious misunderstandings and gags about pubic hair. The audience understands that the truth will out and the transformation of Viola – this man dressed as a woman dressed as a man – is just part of the fun. It's a trick Shakespeare also pulled a couple of years earlier in *As You Like It* (1599), another comic masterpiece where gender is pulled at and teased for the audience's pleasure.

But there's more at stake for Viola. Dressing as a man gives her access to the privileges of the male world, but it also might reflect 'a truer version of the person that Viola/Cesario is but has never before had the opportunity to present', suggests Thomas. Viola goes on to become the object of Olivia's desire. Is she experiencing lesbian love? Or is she finally at home in her temporary trans identity? Or both? On Shakespeare's stage, sex becomes something magical and temporary, as simple as a costume to be put on and taken off again.

Everything is seemingly righted at the end: lovers are united, as are Viola and Sebastian, the genderplay ends and heteronormativity is finally restored. But the characters, and the audience, are forever changed by the experience. In 1992 academic Valerie Traub shocked Shakespeare stans with her collection of essays *Desire and Anxiety: The Circulation of Sexuality in Shakespearean Drama*, pointing out that Viola experiences lesbian eroticism; and Charles Casey's essay 'Gender Trouble in *Twelfth Night*' (1997) goes even further. His theory is that the Viola–Olivia affair, 'along with the homoerotics found in relations between Antonio and Sebastian as well as between Orsino and his page' makes sexuality one of *Twelfth Night*'s major themes. Which is, you know, pretty queer.

In their 2016 essay *Gender & Behavior in Twelfth Night*, American Shakespeare Center puts it clearly: '*Twelfth Night* . . . suggests that, in the view of society, at least, a person's role in life is more defined by what they wear and how they behave than it is by anatomy.' By the end of the play, Viola's costume changes have made her both lesbian (as both Viola and Olivia are female), gay (as both actors would have been male), and gender nonconforming, often all at the same time. As the great RuPaul, truly the Shakespeare of our times, has said: 'We're all born naked, and the rest is drag.'

AKHENATEN

The once-erased rebel pharaoh of Ancient Egypt

Meet the Rebel Pharaoh Akhenaten, unexpected king of Egypt and deathly reformer of the ancient world, with perky breasts, exquisite features and surprisingly wide Earth Mother hips. Ruling from around 1351 to 1334 BCE, Akhenaten was the tenth ruler of the Eighteenth Dynasty, father of Ancient Egyptian megastar Tutankhamun (proven with genetic testing), and perhaps the lover or husband of one Smenkhkare, his son-in-law and wing man. In the years following his rule, he was methodically erased from monuments and paintings; for two millennia Akhenaten was just a whisper in the archives, until archaeological discoveries in the late 1800s put him back into the narrative. There is now evidence of his life and work, but almost all of it is fascinatingly messy, contradictory – with alien conspiracy theories and claims of insanity – and very, very queer.

Akhenaten, born Amenhotep IV, was never meant to be king. His older brother was next in line, but when that brother died unexpectedly the crown came to Akhenaten – and it immediately went to his head. He conjured his own god, Aten, and vanquished all others, making Egypt essentially monotheistic after aeons of its people worshipping fantastical, animal-headed deities. And with this new singular sun god, Akhenaten announced that he was Aten's one true son.

It was this relationship between the pharaoh and his new god that earned Akhenaten his rebel status. He also married the legendary Nefertiti and had six or seven children, with one of his daughters probably married to Smenkhkare, the man whom some historians suggest was Akhenaten's lover. There is ancient art that seems to show Akhenaten embracing another man: is this proof of a gay pharaoh, or was it just part of Akhenaten's cultural redesign, which brought a more expressionistic, loose style to paintings and monuments? Or, as some historians propose, was the man in question Nefertiti herself?

There are gigantic statues (colossi) of Akhenaten, the tallest of which tower at almost 13 metres (42 feet), revealing a unique yet fascinating body. The pharaoh has the swell of small breasts, a feminine face and wide, wide hips. And there is nothing like these statues anywhere else in Egyptian history; pharaohs would always commission super-swole portraits, like gym-mirror selfies, all muscles and bulge, but Akhenaten was different. In 1925, the discovery of these colossi caused scandal among Egyptology geeks who wondered if they were unfortunate mistakes, symbolic interpretation, or perhaps unfiltered glimpses of Akhenaten's true body. One colossus seems to show Akhenaten naked, but without his pharaoh's penis, like an Ancient Egyptian Ken doll.

The colossi have inspired all manner of theories that Akhenaten had a DSD (difference of sex development) and various syndromes; and even that – for those armchair historians who have watched too much *Stargate* – a bulbous skull thought to be Akhenaten's is evidence of his alien origins. 'There is . . . a desire to see "naturalness" in the distinctive iconography of Akhenaten himself,' writes the late Dominic Montserrat in his book *Akhenaten: History, Fantasy and Ancient Egypt* (2000), 'whose body is like no other pharaoh's.' But, in the end, Monserrat reminds his readers that the current consensus is that Akhenaten merely wanted to acknowledge his own mythical status – that of the son of a bisexual sun god – and if he wanted to add boobs and hips, then so be it. Is there perhaps a need for us to wonder about, or try to explain, bodies that might surprise us when we might instead think of them as an expression of some deeper, gendered feeling?

Montserrat allows us another sense-check in his book, underlining that Akhenaten was as much a fantasy figure as he was a living, breathing monarch. In this way, we can imagine that he thought himself a mythical being; and today there are others who certainly think the same. The 'ancient aliens' hypothesis has dogged Egyptologists for decades, with historians having to explain that, no, the pyramids were not created by aliens or superbeings from Atlantis (Monserrat has fun entertaining the different theories, as kooky as old *X-Files* episodes). And for every scholar who writes him off as insane, there is a modern religion that looks to Akhenaten as a messianic figure, even an influencer of Moses.

The Victorians saw Akhenaten as a straight-as-they-come family man, but in the 1910s, Freud became a pharaoh fanboy, and by the 1920s Akhenaten acquired a possibly gay quality. The theory was based on negative misconceptions of gay men; in 1925 historians were bewitched by the feminine appearance of the colossi, but also the new discovery of a stela, or commemorative stone tablet, showing Akhenaten tickling the chin of a man, thought to be Smenkhkare. For some, that was proof enough, and by the late 1920s Akhenaten was as gay as they come. 'He has so often been represented in terms of the hoariest stereotypes of gay men: over-fond of their mothers, artistic and emotionally disturbed,' says Monserrat,

'But he is also caught up in the crusade to find a legitimizing cultural history of gay identity, in which the ancient world plays a vital part.'

Mythical queer superbeing, earthly reformer or ancient gender nonconformer who was nearly erased from history: who knows who the real Akhenaten is? Can we consider him a gay, bisexual or trans hero, or just painfully misunderstood – even insane, like so many historians suggest? An idea at which the queer reader might merely roll their eyes; we've heard that one before.

ODIN

Legendary Norse daddy-god
of eternal female magic

At the US Capitol riots in 2021, the world watched aghast as a rabble of lumpy men and women stormed the sacred halls of democracy. One man, the QAnon Shaman – a sort of protein-powder- and conspiracy-theory-fuelled gym-bro – infamously wandered the stormed Capitol Building, bare-chested in Viking cosplay, with what seem to be Scandinavian tattoos on his torso. One symbol appears to be the valknut, an old Norse 'knot of the dead' symbol sometimes linked to Odin, and another Mjolnir, the legendary hammer belonging to Nordic superbeing Thor – and it set the media world alight. Journalists feverishly reported that ancient Scandi mythology had become the go-to for all manner of far-right dickweeds, especially white supremacists. The valknut is recognized as a hate symbol by the Anti-Defamation League and Mjolnir has appeared on flags at far-right rallies. And for a time, Odin and

Thor, mythical men of ancient times, were thought to have been horribly appropriated.

But the thing about mythical beings is that they are always in flux; they can be magically transformed by myth-lovers who conjure new theories, write new stories and uncover unique facets of their favourite deities. If far-righters and their ilk can repurpose Scandinavian legends for their own nefarious means, then surely the opposite is true too. Enter queer Odin, serving brawn and truculence with chaotic top energy, the gayest god of the Nordic pantheon.

To understand Odin's queerness, one needs to know about seid (we'll get to that) and his place in the pantheon. The great sorcerer of the gods, Odin is the enigmatic, musclebound leader and 'all-father' of the magical Aesir tribe and the heavenly Valhalla, and he thrives on the battlefield. He has two pet ravens, two wolves, rides about on Sleipnir, the flying eight-legged horse-child of Loki (see page 93) and has one eye (the other he gave up absorbing the knowledge of the universe), making him the unofficial god of winking.

'He seems like a classic old white straight man, right?' says Viking scholar and creator of the *Vikings Are Gay* podcast (17 February 2020) Amy Jefford Franks. '[But] we have a number of sources that allude to Odin's gender being a little bit . . . weird.' Jefford Franks points out there are several ancient stories and poems in which Odin is described as 'being queer' by Loki and Thor, no less, and another where Odin disguises himself as a woman.

The source of Odin's queerness seems to be seid, the ecstatic, near-sexual magical force that powered the Nordic legends of the Late Scandinavian Iron Age. Seid, like the Ancient Greek notion of eros, is the sizzling passion behind creativity and physical prowess, but unlike eros, seid is a purely female domain. Which begs the question: what was tough-ass and very male Odin doing being its official master?

Norwegian archaeologist and Odin stan Brit Solli attempts to answer the conundrum in her paper 'Queering the Cosmology of the Vikings' (2008). In it, she wades through the works of discomfited academics of the last hundred years, each too nervous to explore Odin's gender and sexuality. But Solli goes deep: 'men could not practise it [seid] without shame' and yet here was the great brutish king of the gods! 'He is the manliest god of warriors,' she writes, 'but he is also the unmanly master of seid.'

There was a slur word for the male shamans who used female magic: *ergi*, which roughly translates as 'unmanly', 'it basically seems to be bottom-shaming for the Viking age,' says Jefford Franks. Another surprising aspect of Odin was his love of the arts; he is not just a brattish warmonger with massive guns, but also a lover of poetry (in fact, he speaks only in poems). Solli thinks *ergi* might be a sort of stand-in for 'gay', particularly from a modern Western perspective. Or might she mean 'queer'? She points out the strict gender roles of ancient Norse times, and that Odinic shamans might have switched gender to perform seid, if only ceremonially. 'When practising seid, Odin challenged important taboos,' Solli says; 'seid was necessary for the survival of the tribe; hence breaking taboos was necessary. Odin had to be a queer god, because only by his doing seid and being queer could the world continue to exist.' In this way, the great musclebound Odin is a complex figure of duality, using magic to straddle the gender divide with his thick, hairy thighs, and winking while he does it.

With far-righters reclaiming Norse and ancient Scandinavian symbols while at the same time spewing gay and queer slurs at rallies, they seem to have no idea quite how queer the history they are appropriating is. If the QAnon Shaman and far-right bros are indeed investing in Norse tattoos, and invoking Odin while they're at it, they are performing a sort of magical Viking queerness; something very *ergi* indeed.

THE DOCTOR

The gender-regenerating alien Time Lord

Meet the Doctor, an intergalactic yet incredibly English alien Time Lord from the planet Gallifrey, with two big hearts, an eye for social justice, and 'great hair – some really great hair', according to his onetime companion, Rose ('Turn Left', 2008). He bounces chaotically through space and time in his reality-folding spaceship, the TARDIS, fighting tyranny and schooling his human companions in complex metaphysics – i.e., 'a big ball of wibbly wobbly, timey wimey stuff' ('Blink', 2007).

Since its inception in 1963, *Doctor Who* has become deeply embedded in British culture and is the longest-running sci-fi TV show in the world. But the Doctor himself (or herself – the doctor is sometimes female) is an enigmatic, mythic and singular force in his own right. Through a series of magical transformations and his eternal outsider status, he has earned himself a place in the pantheon of queer heroes, with a furiously loyal fanbase to prove it.

Queer people have always had a thing for the Doctor. From the show's early B-movie kitsch and camp look and feel, to its current big budget and super-inclusive format, we have been with the Doctor every step of the way. Some claim there is revisionism at play in imagining the Doctor – first thought up in the early 1960s – as a queer creation. And, even though the family show has, in the past, maintained an overarchingly conservative point of view, there is more than enough in the *DW* canon to certify his rainbow credentials.

For a start, queer creatives have been involved in *Doctor Who* from the beginning, both in front of and behind the camera, and queer stories, both officially and unofficially, glimmer in the subtext. In 1966, Patrick Troughton, the second Doctor, rolled around knowingly with his cute male companion (played by the handsome Frazer Hines), much to the delight of gay and bi viewers. In later seasons, queer characters entered the main plot, from a character inspired by gay icon Alan Turing to brash bisexual Captain Jack Harkness, lesbian companion Bill Potts, and Madame Vastra and Jenny Flint (a sort of lesbian Sherlock and Watson).

In 1994, LGBTQ+ group the Sisterhood of Karn held its first social in a bear bar in London, UK, unashamedly focused on keeping alive the eternal flame of queer *Doctor Who* fandom. More than two decades later, their prayers were answered: in 2005, a reboot opened a universe of possibilities for the Doctor; gay showrunner Russell T Davies took over and famously supercharged the format, repositioning it as a more modern and queer-friendly creation. And in 2020, British Ph.D Mike Stack's survey maintained that *Doctor Who* superfans are ten times more likely to be gay men, making *DW* conventions pretty queer indeed.

In recent times, the Time Lord has ventured even further into the queerverse, itself expanding at an exponential rate. Powered by authors like Juno Dawson, author of a *Doctor Who* novel and several queer audio dramas, and Patrick Ness, who added a gay love story at the queer heart of his *Doctor Who* TV spinoff, *Class* (2016). Every few seasons the Doctor regenerates, taking on a new, usually white, straight male form; but in 2017 he finally became female (played by Jodie Whittaker) and slowly seemed to fall in love with her female companion, Yaz (Mandip Gill), and in 2023 the Doctor's next iteration was realized by Black Scottish-Rwandan actor Ncuti Gatwa.

There are obvious parallels between the Doctor and many of his queer fans. From the Daleks to the Cybermen, there are common monsters to fight, all of them hellbent on universal dominion and either subjugation or sameness – individuals need not apply. And the Doctor himself is an outcast, refusing to conform and shunned by his own society. In the wider context of genre, science fiction, or SF, has traditionally been the space in which exploration of identity is part of the mission, and in *Doctor Who* gender, race and sexuality can be blown apart with zygma beams and fused back together with the Doctor's sonic screwdriver. So, what is the Doctor's response to the Daleks' call to 'exterminate' his uniqueness? It is self-creation, carving a place for himself in space and time, and creating his own 'logical' family of companions, enlisting allies in an otherwise unfriendly universe. Is there anything queerer than that?

FRODO AND SAM

J R R Tolkien's 'Are they . . . you know?' hobbit couple

Ever since J R R Tolkien's two delightfully large-footed male hobbits slipped off their clothes for a skinny-dip, ran through the long grass and lay together naked in the sun, readers have wondered 'Just what it is that makes people think Frodo and Sam might be a gay couple?' As the emotional heart of *The Lord of the Rings* (1954), Tolkien's iconic high-fantasy novel, the relationship between Frodo Baggins, the unlikely hero of Middle Earth, and his gardener, Samwise Gamgee, has inspired and delighted readers and movie fans for decades. But in the anything-is-possible world of wizards, dwarves, elves and the threat of a crushing evil force, queer love between Frodo and Sam has long been thought too outlandish to be true.

In 1999, when historian and Tolkien fan David Craig published his now infamous article 'Queer Lodgings: Gender and Sexuality in *The Lord of the Rings*', which explored Tolkien's

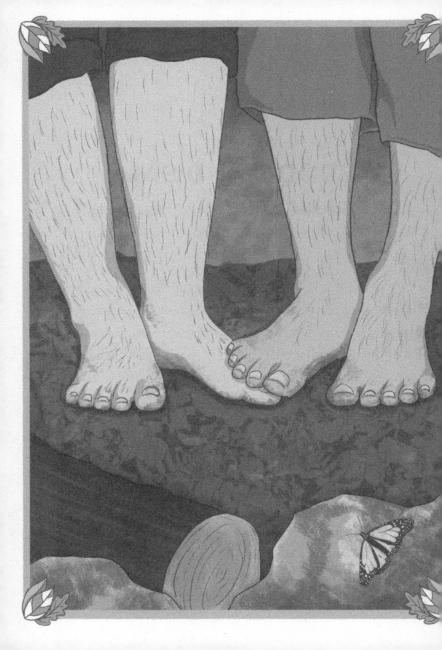

epic and suggested the faintest glimmer of gayness, it didn't go down very well. Everyone from Tolkien traditionalists to Dungeons & Dragons nerds were aghast; one lyrical complaint letter suggested that Craig would 'probably find a doughnut sexual' (Craig later confirmed he does not much care for doughnuts). And even though Peter Jackson's award-winning film franchise (2001–03) had less kissing and handholding and fewer naked embraces between Frodo and Sam than the original text, it did little to dispel the idea that the hobbits' intense love was not 100 per cent brotherly. In the climax of Jackson's *The Return of the King* (2003), Frodo and Sam are about to meet their fate on the smoky slopes of Mount Doom (spoiler: they survive). It is almost impossible not to imagine the heartbreaking scene as a prelude to a kiss, and Frodo and Sam soon launched a thousand 'Is he . . . you know?' queer memes.

Tolkien served at the front in the First World War and had felt both the sharp pain of seeing his friends killed and the intense male bonding between soldiers whose lives are at stake. (Sam is thought to have been inspired by a batman, a low-rank or lower-class soldier who acted as a faithful valet to senior officers.) But warfare is its own sort of nightmarish, fantasy place; and, although it's usually a male domain, in war the traditional idea of gender can be put on hold (anyone who has seen the 2012 US Marine's 'Call Me Maybe' video knows this to be true). Perhaps soldiers like Tolkien returning from war were trying to make sense of their intense relationships and bonds with other men.

Writer Molly Ostertag's essay 'Queer readings of *The Lord of the Rings* are not accidents' (2021) goes further into the *LOTR* queerness quest than Craig's. She carefully explores Tolkien's texts, letters and endless appendices, using evidence of the author's own life and circle of fellow writers, the Inklings, to examine the enduring love between Frodo and Sam. Tolkien had gay and lesbian friends, including W H Auden (who was a big fan of *Rings*), and, as Ostertag says, he would have been aware that 'open same-sex romance was a social and often literal death sentence where even writing about it (except to condemn it) was forbidden'.

In the text, Sam's love for Frodo is deeply physical: 'He is flustered around Frodo,' Ostertag points out, 'blushing when spoken to, holding "and gently stroking" his hands, face, and hair in various situations, and constantly expressing his loyalty.' When they share a bed in another scene, Ostertag counts not one, not two or three, but four kisses shared between the two hobbits. But it is the non-physical – or intense 'spiritual' love, as Craig puts it – that bonds Frodo and Sam and goes on to save the world. Tolkien saw Frodo and Sam in this way too – to him, they weren't lovers, but beings who shared something even greater.

With evil defeated, Frodo and Sam have a heroes' welcome back at home and Sam marries his sweetheart, Rosie. He is torn because he also wants to live with Frodo; but Frodo is suffering from war wounds that refuse to heal, and in the final moments of the book he leaves for the Undying Lands, knowing Sam could never be truly happy watching him suffer. But, as Ostertag points out, they are finally reunited – in the book and the appendices – decades later, with Sam following Frodo after Rosie dies. In this way, Frodo and Sam have the ring of E M Forster's eponymous Maurice and his male lover, Alec; as Craig points out, both couples are finally together in the green woods at the end of their stories.

So, *are* Frodo and Sam . . . you know? Ostertag seems to think it is likely, and Craig says 'it is an irony (although probably one Tolkien would deny) that the love that conquers all is the love that dare not speak its name'. It is important to note that Tolkien did not intend for his handholding hobbits-in-love to be thought of as gay – not in any modern sense; but the one power the reader has is to make up their own mind. Although it is true that there is sometimes an aspect of revisionism in queering the past (not every literary figure – gender-nonconforming hobbit or not – can be a hidden gay, trans, or nonbinary treasure), sometimes there is indeed queer gold in them there hills.

THE SANDMAN

The queer hero of Neil Gaiman's super-gay epic

To understand the work of British fantasy writer Neil Gaiman is to imagine him as a sort of literary deity. He has hordes of loyal devotees who celebrate his award-winning novels, comics, films and TV adaptations through fanfiction, clever cosplay, merch, tattoos – and even feverish online discussions about his fountain pens (his favourites include the Pilot Custom 823). From the beginning, Gaiman's world-building has been expansive, surprising and inclusive, so it's no accident that both his literary creations and fans can sometimes be very queer indeed.

Gaiman's fandom means his characters have almost instant mythical status. This is most obvious in his novel *American Gods* (2001), where he riffs on well-known ancient deities from Ganesha to Odin, pitching them against new creations like Media and Technical Boy, a creepy childlike god of the internet. But it is *Gods'* predecessor *The Sandman* (1989–96),

Gaiman's series of beloved horror-fantasy comics, published by DC throughout the early 1990s, that arguably mark the author out as a sort of queer myth-making auteur.

The Sandman, aka Dream, is one of the Endless: seven elemental beings who are manifestations of human ideas and experiences, from Destruction to Desire. But it is Dream who is the tragic hero of the tale: his task is to rebuild his fallen kingdom and save the waking world while he's at it with the help and hinderance of his siblings. Like many of Gaiman heroes, he is coded as queer, a visionary outcast with Goth styling (and the author's own hair), but he represents just a fraction of the complex approach to gender and sexuality in *The Sandman* universe. Across 75 comics, readers meet the Corinthian, a gay antagonist, Wanda Mann, a trans woman, and all manner of painfully cool bisexuals in a radical cast of characters that feels oddly prescient for the early 1990s. 'When I was writing it – and today – I had gay friends and I had trans friends,' Gaiman told *The Queer Review* in 2022. 'I wanted to see them represented in the comics that I was writing and it felt to me like if I wrote comics and left them out, then I wouldn't be representing my world, or the world that I was in, or the world I was perceiving accurately, bravely, or truly. And that's the point of art.'

More than 30 years after the first *Sandman* comic, Gaiman's TV adaptation premiered in 2022 with a few noticeable tweaks that left viewers (many of whom have been longtime fans of the work) fizzing at its new, 'everyone is gay' approach. It is the queerest manifestation of Gaiman's *Sandman* yet, with the return of antagonist the Corinthian (who actor Boyd Holbrook suggests is now more pansexual than gay), and bisexual Johanna Constantine (freshly out of a lesbian relationship, cynical, and obsessed with the occult, no less). The cleverest update is the character Desire, genderfluid, sexy and sinuous in the comics, and officially nonbinary in the TV adaptation, played by nonbinary actor Mason Alexander Park. It all suggests that squaring the 1990s *Sandman* with contemporary queer culture, with its evolving lexicon, has been easy.

Perhaps the most radical aspect of *The Sandman*'s queerness – in both the 1990s comics and its TV adaptation – is that nothing feels particularly worthy or educational. Some contemporary queer stories can, at times, be vehicles only for representation rather than spellbinding yarns, but Gaiman seems to assume the best of his audience and simply gets on with the story. His characters are free to be as complicated and conflicted as they like, their queerness important but not always essential to their being. Seeing oneself on the page or on screen is powerful, but Gaiman shows us what it is like when done unselfconsciously (although with a 1990s Goth sensibility). *The Sandman* TV adaptation marked something of an evolution in how queer people are represented in mainstream drama; it is a big-budget gay-fest of a show with an incredibly diverse cast that shows we can be anything, from landlords and gardeners to occult detectives, interdimensional beings and beyond. Most importantly, we can be as good or as bad as we like. As Gaiman has pointed out in one of his online fan forums: 'Godlike things are just as likely to be screwed up, wrongheaded and mistaken as anyone else.'

THE MINOAN BROTHERHOOD

The post-Stonewall gay witches of 1970s New York

Meet Eddie Buczynski (1947–89), radical firebrand and founder of the Minoan Brotherhood, the esoteric and super-queer magical mystery society at the centre of 1970s countercultural New York. Inspired by ancient Cretan myths and Minoan beliefs, contemporary Wicca and its lack of gay and bisexual acceptance, he set about creating some of his own queer magic – and he did just that.

A working-class New Yorker, Buczynski took aspects of his parents' Roman Catholic beliefs and, according to writer Michael G Lloyd, remixed them with the ancient myths and legends of Ancient Greece and Egypt, performing his own rituals at home. As a child he was bullied at school – the gay man's rite of passage of the time – and in his twenties, during the mid-1960s, he moved from Queens to Greenwich Village. It was the epicentre of the counterculture movement, the embattled gay community and burgeoning pagan and Wiccan belief. There, Buczynski met handsome Leo Martello, a Wiccan priest who, after the Stonewall riots and the summer of 'gay power' in 1969, had become a prominent gay-rights activist. It was Martello who introduced Buczynski to his first love, burly bear and witch Herman Slater, and in 1972 the pair opened The Warlock Shop together in New York's Brooklyn Heights.

It was through one of their first employees, artist Ted Carey, that Buczynski first intersected with NYC royalty. Carey was friend to Candy Darling and Andy Warhol and The Warlock Shop became synonymous with NYC cool. 'He was just magical,' said his onetime high priestess Lady Rhea in her 2016 interview with fellow witch Reverend Alexander Cabot. 'His appearance, these intense green eyes, his long gorgeous red hair, and this hot masculine body . . . all the women and all the men had a crush on Eddie.' Although Buczynski was both a big warlock on the magic scene and a big hit on the gay scene, he found his sexuality at odds with some of the pagan groups of New York. There are countless pathways and traditions towards pagan and Wiccan belief, but many include a ritualized focus on male and female, and maintaining balance between the two, which can create a sort of gender-essentialist aspect that, in the 1970s, seemed to exclude gay, lesbian, bisexual and trans followers.

Buczynski discovered that the world of magic was not immune to anti-gay attitudes. He started to look back to the original 'Mother Goddess cults' of antiquity for inspiration, but none of them seemed quite right. In the end, he found solace in the Ancient Minoan religion. In Michael G Lloyd's book *Bull of Heaven: The Mythic Life of Eddie Buczynski and the Rise of the New York Pagan* (2012) he quotes Buczynski on finally founding a new coven or 'grove' just for gay and bisexual men: '. . . sick of all the shit flying back and forth from coven to coven (mainly concerning me) . . . I decided that, in order to find fulfilment in my religious beliefs, I must find a pagan cult which would welcome me as I am – a proud gay man.' The group, a sort of mystery cult, thrived with gay men who had always dreamed of practising the craft, and with Buczynski focused on 'celebrating life through male love'.

Buczynski liked to stir the cauldron. As a fiery coven leader and outspoken activist, he moved between rival covens seeking more training and initiations, and he broke more than a few hearts on his way to becoming a major figure in the gossipy witch wars of New York pagan society. The Minoan Brotherhood grew, and soon the Minoan Sisterhood was formed, with Buczynski continuing his studies and reading archaeology at Bryn Mawr College.

The Minoan Brotherhood and Eddie's own magical story is also the tale of gay New York, from bears and bathhouses, the Stonewall riots, Warhol celebs and The Warlock Shop, through to the Aids epidemic in the 1980s, which affected the Minoan Brotherhood and eventually Buczynski himself. He passed away in 1989 but not before handing in his dissertation on Minoan artifacts and travelling to Crete, the birthplace of Minoan magic. The Brotherhood lives on with some 30 groves across the world, a community that is underpinned by some of the early members, who advocate study, mental discipline and keeping Buczynski's dream alive.

THE VALKYRIES

The heartbreaking Norse harbingers of lesbian doom

On 8 July 2022, the world echoed with the sad sound of a million lesbian hearts breaking. It was finally release day for the Marvel movie *Thor: Love and Thunder*, the hotly anticipated retro-toned comic-fantasy masterpiece that, for queer people, promised one extraordinary thing: lesbian Valkyrie. The character played by actor Tessa Thompson, a no-nonsense warrior woman and King of Asgard, had long been a PQI (Person of Queer Interest). Ever since rumours abounded that Valkyrie's canon bisexual scene in *Thor: Ragnarok* (2017) had been cut from the movie, queer chatter had tantalized lesbian and bisexual Marvel fans who thus expected something rather special in return in *Love and Thunder* (the king finally meeting her queen, perhaps?). But they were sorely disappointed. A minor flirtation between Valkyrie and a Greek goddess and a brief mourning for a lost love (aka the Lesbian Tragedy trope) was all that the lesbians were gifted. No wonder their hearts broke.

Valkyries have long been thought of as the noble warriors of Odin (see page 169), his tough but ethereal maiden-force who would kindly guide the big, one-eyed magical muscle-daddy's dead heroes from the battlefields to a comfortable and well-earned eternal paradise at Valhalla, the great hall of chosen ones. As horse-loving 'chooser[s] of the slain', Valkyries would swish their man-slaying swords and, despite their butch vibes, there are also epic stories of them swishing their hair, offering reviving mead, and falling in love with mortal men. This loving, booze-pouring and life-giving version of the Valkyries is one of the most enduring.

But Norse-myth geek Daniel McCoy and his book *The Viking Spirit* (2016) remind us that the earliest Valkyrie stories tell a different tale. To the original scribes these are hellish shadow creatures, foreboders of war, and more connected to the realm of the dead than the land of the living. These death demons might not have guided the lost souls of heroes but rather feasted on their dying bodies. In fact, evidence of the Valkyries predates mentions of Valhalla, which itself may have alluded to the more recent Christian idea of heaven. Put this way, the Valkyries would have swooped in, munched on your bones and dragged what's left of you to Hel (the Norse/pagan underworld). McCoy points to a gruesome poem within *Njál's Saga* from the 13th century. In it, 12 Valkyries weave the 'tragic fate' of the warriors using 'intestines for their thread, severed heads for weights . . . all the while chanting their intentions with ominous delight'. With modern lesbians having long embraced cottage-core and crafting, this seems – as McCoy says – ominous indeed.

Marvel's Valkyrie, she who has so much lesbian potential, first appeared in the Avenger comics as Brunnhilde in 1970, leader of the Lady Liberators. But she wasn't quite the character who went on to pique queer interest. Instead, she was the male writers' snarky joke: an aggressive and misogynistic take on early 1970s feminism (who turned out to be the evil Enchantress in disguise anyway). She was transformed in 1973 under writer Steve Englehart, and joined Marvel's *Defenders* fully fledged with confidence, impressive might and a growing queer edge, keeping the male characters' sexism in check. She reappeared in the comics throughout the decades, taking human host bodies, fighting evil, and flying about on a Scottish Pegasus named Mr Horse, and eventually had her first gay kiss with Indiana Jones-styled archaeologist Annabelle Riggs in *The Fearless Defenders* (2013), an all-too-brief relationship that ended in Annabelle sacrificing herself and becoming yet another Valkyrie host body (more Lesbian Tragedy).

And yet, Marvel's is not the only alternative version of the mythical women. Alongside age-old horror poems about weaving with the guts of their victims, archaeological finds across Scandinavia suggest that the ancient ones were just as excited about Valkyries as we are in contemporary times. Digs have uncovered Valkyrie amulets and figurines, in celebration or perhaps in fearful appeasement. And Odin's warrior maidens have long been the subject of art, in music like Richard Wagner's opera *Der Ring des Nibelungen*, in literature (Valkyries guest-star in Hans Christian Anderson's *The Marsh King's Daughter*), and in video games, as well as through Tessa Thompson's sizzling queer superhero creation.

'Whether in their loving or bloodthirsty modalities,' says McCoy, Valkyrie have endured hundreds of years of evolution – from their demonic beginnings to the swishy-haired life-giving maidens commemorated in amulets and figurines, to the intergalactic and fair-minded warrior of Marvel comics and movies. Perhaps one day lesbians will be given what they have been waiting for, a truly gay storyline for their hero of queer myth; one heart-mending, life-changing ride of the Valkyrie.

THE WILD THINGS

Maurice Sendak's burly untamed monsters of Fire Island

To sun-kissed Fire Island, New York, the legendary beach-fringed wonderland just a train or ferry ride from Manhattan, where queer people – mainly gay men – might escape the oppressive city heat and stifling straight expectations as they slip into a pair of Speedos and give themselves over to the wilds. The 32-mile-long island, car-free and just two or three blocks wide, has been an unofficial summer spot for queer people since the 1930s. And it was here, in the early 1960s, that Maurice Sendak (1928–2012), legendary gay Jewish author-illustrator, wrote his most famous and beloved children's picture book, *Where the Wild Things Are* (1963). In the story, Max – a tantrum-prone little boy in a wolf costume – is banished to his room, which transforms magically into a jungle island where he meets, befriends and becomes king of the Wild Things, hairy, thick-set monsters who live by their own rules. Eventually, Max finds his way home after learning how to master the wild.

Sendak grew up in lower-middle-class Brooklyn in a large Yiddish-speaking family, mourning relatives in Poland lost during the Holocaust and weathering the Depression, the Second World War and the immigrant experience. Danger always seemed close by and Sendak behaved accordingly (his mother would call him *vilde chaya* meaning 'wild animal'). By his teenage years he knew he was gay; there was something wild within him and he dreaded the thought of being pushed outside his small Jewish immigrant community. Sendak came out in 2008, when he was 80 years old.

We can thank academic Golan Moskowitz for charting Sendak's artistic and sexual evolution in his book *Wild Visionary* (2020) and for shining a queer light on the Wild Things themselves. Moskowitz sees Sendak very much in a 'queer Jewish context'; he was both gay and gender nonconforming (in that he was a sensitive man in overtly macho times), and had immigrant heritage – he didn't quite fit in. But, as Moskowitz points out, although an artist's work 'shouldn't be reduced or defined by the artist's identity alone', Sendak is rarely thought of in terms of his queerness or Jewishness.

Sendak's superpower was to recall the past and give it shape – he had a psychic hotline to the loves, fears and feverish mood swings of childhood – and it was this that informed his work. *Where the Wild Things Are* is one of more than 90 celebrated Sendak titles, with more than 30 million copies sold in the US. And in a lecture in 2021, Moskowitz pointed to Sendak's often 'bold depictions of decidedly non-Anglo-Saxon protagonists'.

Sendak thought of his work as autobiographical and, as Moskowitz points out, queerness and Jewishness glimmers on almost every page. His Wild Things are echoes of his Jewish aunts, uncles and cousins, 'Those relatives would grab you and twist your face, and they thought that was an affectionate thing to do,' Sendak told *The Jewish Chronicle* in 2009. 'And children can be so cruel. My brother, sister and I would laugh at those people, who we, of course, grew up to love very much. But that's who the wild things are. Foreigners, lost in America without a language.' And, although he wasn't officially out, Sendak did not shy away from responding to gay social issues and collaborating with other queer creatives. His controversial *We're All in the Dumps with Jack and Guy* (1993) is an incredibly brave, Aids-themed children's picture book published at the height of the Aids epidemic. A friend of Sendak, quoted in *The New Yorker* in 2013, said that Jack represented Sendak's beloved late brother and that Guy was his partner of 50 years, Eugene Glynn.

But back to that summer in the early 1960s, a few nautical miles from both Manhattan and the Brooklyn of Sendak's youth. What autobiographical inspirations did Fire Island allow him, and which hairy, thick-bodied creatures wandered the groves? Was it his own Jewish childhood that expressed itself on the page, his teenage queerness, or something else?

EZILÍ DANTOR

The lesbian protector spirit of ancient Haitian Vodou

A splash of rum on the ground, perfume and candlelight, a royal-blue cloth and a belief in the queer magic of Vodou are the best ways to honour the deity Ezilí Dantor, ancient and feisty protector of lesbians. In 2016, award-winning writer Beenish Ahmed met a series of Haitian queer Vodou communities for the magazine *The Advocate*. There, in Port-au-Prince, she found small, defiant groups of queer Vodouizants, tyrannized by society but fearless in their devotion to queer-friendly and 'deux-manières' or double-gendered spirits. Through Ezilí Dantor and other beings, they had rediscovered the age-old religion and made it their own.

Traditionally, there is a magical stretchiness to Vodou, where deities like Ezilí are not fixed but malleable, with different devotees calling on her for health, happiness, protection and more. In the 1980s and 1990s she was the favoured spirit of single mothers, but now queer love is her domain. But who is Ezilí Dantor, and how did she become a saint-like figure to the queer people of Haiti?

As the main lwa, or spirit, of Haitian Vodou, Ezilí Dantor is one of hundreds of deities with roots in ancient West Africa, transported with enslaved people to the Americas. There, the Roman Catholicism enforced by French colonialists pressed down on the Vodou tradition in the hopes of stamping it out. Instead, it became absorbed and reinterpreted, creating something both novel and ancient. And the forced diaspora also created a new, multicultural African community where previously separate groups shared their own beliefs, and Vodou lwa gained new facets and powers.

Ezilí Dantor has a connection with images of the Black Madonna of Czestochowa, the famous Catholic icon that was brought to Haiti by Polish mercenaries who fought on both sides of the 1802 Haitian Revolution. 'Vodou practitioners identified with this powerful, dark-skinned Madonna,' say Dr Kate Kingsbury and Debra Van Neste in their 2020 essay *How the Polish Black Madonna Became Haitian Vodou Spirit Erzulie Dantor* for Patheos.com (2018), 'merging her into their pantheon of lwa, and meshing her with Ezilí Dantor.' At the time, it was 'most dangerous to worship images of African lwa', they point out; the Black Madonna was a useful stand-in for Ezilí for enslaved people who were living under the cruelty of plantation life.

Although kind, compassionate and sweetly protective like the Catholic Madonna figure, Ezilí is her own being. She is a 'hot spirit', sensuous and strong, and linked to creativity, anger, passion and sex. 'She is a matroness of the LGBT community in Haiti and for many Haitian-Americans in cities such as Miami and New York,' say Kingsbury and Van Neste. 'In particular, she is said to be the defender of lesbians, while her sister, Ezilí Freda, is the matron of gay men, especially drag queens.'

In Haiti, as Ahmed discovered, queer people seek the protection of Ezilí Dantor, spiritual or otherwise. With LGBTQ+ Haitians perennially under threat of discrimination being written into law, social attitudes towards queerness remain hostile, with raids on LGBTQ+ non-profits and casual street violence focused mainly on lesbians and femme-presenting trans people. And with Vodou itself frowned upon by wider society, queer devotion to Ezilí is a dangerous act. But still, there is resistance: 'We have spirits in the sky who like both men and women,' explains a male 'LGBT Vodouizant' to Ahmed. 'It's not considered a bad thing for them, so why would this be a bad thing for us?'

Under the threat of violence, humiliation and the cold shoulder of social shunning, queer Vodou in Haiti has helped create a sense of belonging. But perhaps its most potent effect has been to unleash the magical power of queer joy in Port-au-Prince. Ahmed found that Vodou ceremonies embraced not only Ezilí Dantor, but also drinking and dancing, midnight kisses and music, and the fizzing excitement and camaraderie of queer people letting loose.

SIR LANCELOT

The valiant knight of a legendary bisexual three-way

Now to Camelot and the mythical court of King Arthur, the heroic Celtic Briton and star of countless ancient epic poems and fantastical stories, and the love interest of one handsome and gallant knight, Sir Lancelot. Were the two mythical men brothers-in-arms, sharing a deep, homosocial affection for one another, or did Lancelot long to help Arthur polish his magical sword, Excalibur?

The much-loved Arthurian legends are a sort of past-times soap opera of ancient England, with the king navigating an impossible storyline of invaders, murder plots, illicit affairs and magical foes with the help of his trusted men, a burly dude-crew of knights and Merlin the wizard, sworn to protect their king and his realm. King Arthur and the Knights of the Round Table manage to create a sort of bro-utopia of chivalrous, back-slapping men until the discovery of

Lancelot's affair with Arthur's queen, Guinevere – and then the frat party is over.

From the 12th century, there have been countless adaptations of the Arthurian legends, from Sir Thomas Malory's *Le Morte d'Arthur* (1485) to Tennyson's *Idylls of the King* (1859–85), where Lancelot is perfectly Victorian: courteous and moralistic (until that snitch Merlin blows his cover). Author T H White's first Arthurian novel, *The Sword and the Stone* (1938) and his hugely popular collection of Camelot works *The Once and Future King* (1958) – the *Game of Thrones* of its day – set a new pace for interpretations of Lancelot. Influenced by Malory and Freudian theories, White allowed an early glimmer of gayness in the text, but not in a particularly progressive way. He cast Lancelot as a heroic hot mess – a jealous, ugly turncoat – and subtly implied that he was in love with Arthur. To White, it was Lancelot's queerness that made him such a difficult, unlikable character. After his death in 1964, biographers and friends of White proposed that he might have been gay himself, but with White being troubled, a heavy drinker and several times almost married, had they come to the same conclusion about queerness as had the author himself?

In SFF writer Diana Hurlburt's essay 'T.H. White, Lancelot, and Threesomes' (2013), she points to Marion Zimmer Bradley's humungous *The Mists of Avalon* (1983) as finishing what White had started. In the novel, which has Morgaine aka Morgan Le Fay as its protagonist, Bradley took 'the implied affection between Arthur and his finest knight and wrote it large', with 'Lancelet', Arthur and 'Gwenhwyfar' getting mythical together in a tent; a legendary three-way that made the knight's queerness obvious.

At the time, Bradley's overtly bisexual 'Lancelet' seemed controversial, but Hurlburt writes that 'shades of male homosexual desire and action are found throughout the Arthurian canon'. The ancient stories chart an idealized version of male–male love, allowing the knights some lusty horseplay, Sir Gawain 'smoochies' (as Hurlburt puts it) with the Green Knight, and master of dad-jokes 'Sir Dinadan, "lover of all valiant knights," makes great joy with Sir Palomides in a shared bed.' And in the anonymous 13th-century French prose version of the story, the *Lancelot-Grail*, the young, handsome knight is paired up with older, half-giant King Galehaut, who becomes besotted with him – leading some scholars to wonder if it might be the best (and first?) medieval portrait of the classic bear-twink relationship.

In 2008, the BBC produced a different take with fantasy drama *Merlin*, reimagining Arthur and Lancelot's wizard friend as a young, spindly geek and focusing on his burgeoning friendship with hot blond jock Arthur. Over 65 episodes,

Lancelot is pushed to the side as the show concentrates on the young wizard and king. Fans quickly noted its queer potential, reading Merlin's hidden magical powers as gay and his relationship with Arthur as more than brotherly love. The final episode, with its professions of male–male love, seemed almost to give the fans just what they had been hoping for – and if the growing online fanfic erotica starring the knights of old is anything to go by, queer interest in the Arthurian legends has more to give.

In recent times, much work has been done on queering Camelot, unpicking the ancient stories and examining the queer evolution of its characters. We might look on these mythical men as gay BFFs, medieval male lovers, or simply dedicated friends, but with the ongoing tradition of new Arthurian fantasy and YA fiction, we can look forward to more queer knights at the Round Table.

YARA GREYJOY

The sex-positive butch and accidental poet of *Game of Thrones*

Lesbians and poetry go hand in hand, from the quiet eroticism of Sappho to the passion and pain of Audre Lorde. We can now add a new name to that list: Yara Greyjoy, whose lyrical mastery glows from the pages and glitters on screen in the TV adaptation of George R R Martin's fantasy epic *Game of Thrones* (2011–19). 'Since it's my last night ashore . . .' she declares to her younger brother Theon Greyjoy, 'I'm going to suck the tits off this one.' Known for her plain speaking and crude one-liners, this lesbian lyricist is as subtle as an iron broadsword crunching through the spine of her enemies.

Martin's award-winning novel *A Game of Thrones* (1996) is the first book in his almost-endless *A Song of Fire and Ice* series and slow-burned its way to number one on *The New York Times* Best Sellers list in 2011. His tale of three noble families warring their way through the seven kingdoms of love, sex and dragons inspired the cultish HBO TV adaptation that premiered in 2011. Yara Greyjoy – known as Asha in Martin's books – is the very queer 'reaver' and warrior; raised as a surrogate son by her cantankerous king father, she clomps over the gender boundaries of the incredibly patriarchal *GoT* world to command her own ship, lead her own fighting force and become a major player across two continents.

There are echoes of the real-life Empress Matilda (1102–1167) in Yara, King Henry I of England's only daughter and sole heir after the death of his son, William Adelin. Henry commanded that the throne would one day belong to her; but after his death, Matilda's cousin Stephen of Blois usurped her, and the should-be queen set off to claim her birth right with her own army. Like Matilda, Yara Greyjoy is always off on her own military campaigns to save her brother or protect her homeland.

Much of the appeal of Yara (played by British actor Gemma Whelan) is her queerness; she is unerringly butch, delights in having sex with women, and exists somewhat outside *GoT*'s hetero hot mess of broken hearts, melted heads and chopped-off manhoods. Yet she remains powerful, self-possessed and full of sass. In another story, Yara might be an outcast, but in *GoT* she is formidable. In the novels, Yara Greyjoy's sexuality is unclear, but Whelan has described her as pansexual, saying in an interview in 2016: 'I reckon she's any way. I don't think she'd limit herself to one or the other.'

Sex and sexuality are an integral part of the *GoT* world, but queer viewers have often been frustrated by Martin and HBO's LGBTQ+ storylines. Lesbian and gay sex scenes are fleeting and, importantly, there is no enduring queer relationship; a heavy burden for Yara's strong shoulders. Before *Queer Eye*, a somewhat unknown Jonathan Van Ness's *Gay of Thrones* fan podcast touched on the show's ability to get it wrong. In Season 7, fans fizzed with excitement over Yara's onscreen kiss with Ellaria (Indira Varma), previewed tantalizingly on a trailer ahead of the episode's release, but were furious when they discovered that it was Ellaria's final episode, thus thwarting all chance of lesbian love flourishing on screen.

Queer controversy dogged *GoT* throughout its run, with its beloved lesbian, gay and bisexual characters meeting gruesome and tragic ends. Bisexual Oberyn Martell has his head horrifyingly squished by chunky muscleman the Mountain; Renly Baratheon is killed by a shadow monster (swiftly and unceremoniously in a tent); and Loras Tyrell suffers terribly before being snuffed out himself. The scenes *seemed* to fall under the Bury Your Gays trope but here – again – Yara triumphs. She is a master tactician, avoiding danger as much as she runs towards it; she not only survives but thrives, outlasting all the other queer characters. Perhaps Yara's poetic powers lend her the queer strength she needs to defeat the *GoT* men who stand in her way. As she memorably and devastatingly says, 'Anything with a cock is easy to fool.'

XENA AND GABRIELLE

The legendary warrior princess and her Sapphic soulmate

Truly the love story of the 1990s: the fateful pairing of a statuesque warrior princess and her female soulmate sidekick as they battle sexism, misogyny and heteronormative horrors across an ancient and magical world. For six spellbinding television series, *Xena: Warrior Princess* (1995–2001), itself a spinoff of *Hercules: The Legendary Journeys* (1995–99), captivated its audience with its textual reworkings of Greek myths, stunning New Zealand landscapes and scantily clad cast. The show's female protagonist, Xena (played with gruff warlord rigour by Lucy Lawless), and Gabrielle, her naive and sweet-natured sidekick (played by Renee O'Connor), carried the show to unexpected success, out-performing *Hercules* and earning itself an incredibly loyal fanbase. Much like Peter Jackson's *Lord of the Rings* film and TV franchise, *Xena: Warrior Princess* transformed the creative industries of

New Zealand and created one of the world's first digital communities. In the mid- to late 1990s, fantasy superfans were freshly online via dial-up modems at home or at school, meeting in forums to discuss the show's monsters and magic. Today, digital 'slash' or 'femslash' communities of fanfiction writers who reimagine romantic female and queer popular-culture relationships can trace their roots back to original *Xena* fandom. But in those early days of *Xena* and AOL geek-outs, fans began to wonder: were the warrior princess and Gabrielle really just gal pals?

Queerness on screen was a relatively new concept in the mid-1990s and commercial TV networks, naturally risk-averse, were uneasy. In 1997, Ellen DeGeneres's famous coming-out episode of her hit show *Ellen* was the result of months of negotiation with her network ('Can't Ellen just get a puppy instead?' they asked). In the end, the two-parter attracted 42 million viewers and an Emmy, but also advertiser boycotts and threats from religious groups – and the show was cancelled after its fifth season.

As *Xena* show-makers Rob Tapert and Sam Raimi drew on Taiwanese action-horror star Brigitte Lin for inspiration, flooding the show with *Evil Dead* director Raimi's passion for violence and gore, the network was already somewhat on edge. Queer love and desire between Xena and Gabrielle would have to be kept firmly under the radar, but with the help of Lawless and O'Connor, Tapert and Raimi made sure that *Xena*'s lesbian subtext was deafeningly loud.

When they weren't slaying monsters, decimating armies and undoing ancient curses, Xena and Gabrielle were kissing and hugging, co-parenting, dancing together sexily in leather for the devil and sharing naked massages in the bath. 'We both have families we were born into,' says Xena to her soulmate's expectant, moon-eyed face, 'but sometimes families change, and we have to build our own. For me, our friendship binds us closer than blood ever could.' Xena's now famous 'We are family' speech to Gabrielle is one of the show's countless moments of queer love, much like the sunset scene where Xena presents Gabrielle with an ancient scroll, a poem to show her dear friend how deeply valued she is. The poet? Sappho of Lesbos.

If *Xena*-queerness was officially banned from the screen, it hadn't gone unnoticed elsewhere. In the mid-1990s, struggling car manufacturer Subaru switched up its ailing US marketing strategy to focus on niche groups, rugged outdoorsy types they knew loved their sturdy, spacious but rather uncool models. They coded their commercials to attract one of their target demographics, lesbians, and released an image of a Subaru with a kayak on the roof rack and a licence plate that read XENA LVR (sales soon improved).

In fact, we can thank the lesbians, Subaru-owning and otherwise, for keeping Xena and Gabrielle somewhat in the public consciousness. New generations have also discovered the show, fuelling ongoing debates surrounding the pair's sexual identities, and even creating new content (YouTube is awash with lesbian supercuts of Xena and Gabrielle's gayest moments). Queer fandom is also the cornerstone of both Lawless and O'Connor's acting careers and the actors continue to talk reverently about the show and their onetime characters. Fans who are fresh to the genre have charted how Xena and Gabrielle's relationship is depicted throughout the seasons, from being what seems to be an inside joke to becoming the emotional heart of the show. As Xena battles her own demons (literal and otherwise), Gabrielle's character quietly evolves; she becomes a queer warrior herself.

There is some regret, though. In the final episodes, something irrevocable happens, and what becomes another step in Xena's existence ends her relationship with Gabrielle forever. Fans were distraught at the pair's unhappy ending; and in the decades since, some of the show's makers and actors have expressed sadness in not giving the fans what they needed. But Xena and Gabrielle's relationship is still something to marvel over, a lesbian TV duo years ahead of its time with queer acceptance waving out proudly from the subtext. Looking back at *Xena: Warrior Princess* from a contemporary perspective, we might wonder if it is Xena, Gabrielle, or us who is most transformed by the queerest love of all.

WILLOW AND TARA

The 1990s mall-Goth witches who inspired a generation of queer creativity

'Do you think I chose to be like this?' asks Buffy. She comes out in Season 2 of the cult fantasy-horror TV show and finally tells her mother the truth: yes, she's a vampire slayer. 'It's because you didn't have a strong father figure, isn't it,' her mother worriedly responds, unable to comprehend her teenage daughter's messianic role in protecting humankind from the hellmouth and all the undead horror that lies behind it. And Buffy, like so many queer kids, is thrown out of home.

From its first episode in 1997, *Buffy the Vampire Slayer* has been watched and loved by millions. The supernatural drama follows its heroine (played by Sarah Michelle Geller), fascinating in her apparent normalness, as she balances school and personal life with her true calling: kicking the undead's ass. The show's irreverent, post-modern sense of humour, American high-school antics, feminism and existential philosophizing made it the cult hit of the late 1990s and 2000s, spawning a series of spinoff shows and companion comics. Its fantastical elements and offhand approach to genre allowed for all manner of surprises, and the show's popularity emboldened its creative team to go where no one had gone before. While other 1990s fantasy TV shows like *Xena: Warrior Princess* were queer in subtext only, *Buffy* characters Willow Rosenberg (played by Alyson Hannigan) and Tara Maclay (Amber Benson) were radically out and proud. The teenage witches made history as the first long-term lesbian relationship on US television, and their first kiss, plus Willow's sex scene with Kennedy (we'll get to that), were significant cultural moments. Hannigan and Benson have spoken about the fan letters they received from queer fans at the time.

In the early seasons, there is something comfortingly vanilla about Willow. She's something of a nerd, wears awful outfits, and is both the brains and moral backbone of the group, known as the Scooby Gang. Her queer transformation occurs when she meets Tara in an after-school club of pretend witches. To Willow's surprise, she falls for her, declaring her love a few episodes later. The depiction of their burgeoning lesbian relationship was another TV first: it is gradual, sensitive and authentic, with no shock reveals or pained coming-out scenes. What's more, their queerness isn't seen as a symptom of self-loathing; they are simply two girls (well, witches) in love.

Perhaps there was something about Willow's innocent edge – all fluffy sweaters and snuggles with plushie toys – and her slow lesbian evolution that allowed 1990s America to accept her queerness? She certainly gets away with some racy gay dialogue. In Season 7, the Scooby Gang call on Willow to perform an impossible magical feat. 'This goes beyond anything I've ever done,' she warns, 'it's a total loss of control. And not in a nice wholesome my-girlfriend-has-a-pierced-tongue kind of way.'

In Season 6, inexplicably, Tara is killed. It did not go down well with the fans, not at all. In Judith L Tabron's essay 'Girl on Girl Politics: Willow / Tara and New Approaches to Media Fandom' (2004) she writes that 'Tara's death . . . resulted in one of the great fan outcries . . . thousands of fans mounted an organized protest . . . The fans who complained about Tara's death were often part of internet groups organized specifically around the delights of watching a happy lesbian relationship on television.'

In her grief, the character turns into the terrifying Dark Willow, with black contacts and 1990s mall-Goth clothing, causing havoc until she can be brought back to the not-so-straight and narrow. When she finally meets Kennedy in

Season 7, a trainee slayer and brattish, out lesbian, their relationship is quite different. Willow is no longer sweetly vanilla but passionate, confident and sex-positive; she is now a whole other type of queer woman (for those interested, fan-made supercuts of their sex scene are on YouTube, often to an Evanesence or Nick Lachey soundtrack).

Buffy's long-term effect on popular culture, TV drama, fandom and even academia is immense. Its endless and artful SFF story arcs – novel at the time – can now be felt in similar shows from *Doctor Who* to *Stranger Things*, but *Buffy the Vampire Slayer*'s true legacy might be its own brand of witchy queer acceptance. As a queer teen, seeing yourself on screen is something that stays with you. To a generation of lesbians, for whom *Buffy*'s two young witches were no small aspect of their sexual awakening, Willow Rosenberg and Tara Maclay magically live on.

Mythical queer thanks to. . .

Briony Gowlett, Max Edwards, Leanne Bryan, Mel Four, Caroline Alberti, Jade Moore, Monica Hope, Susanne Hillen, Ilker Hepkaner, Avinash Rajagopal, Gabriella Gershenson, Bernie Kravitz, Shelly Cornick, Jack Bootle, Toby Roberts and Tom McDonald.